Finding Your Maximum Happiness

A Study of the Ten Commandments

Wilbur Glenn Williams

Wesleyan Publishing House
Indianapolis, Indiana

Table of Contents

Finding Your Maximum Happiness

Maximum happiness! That's the subject of this study. How does one get it? After one gets it, how is it kept? If one had it and lost it, how is it regained? These are questions we will try to answer.

Basically, everyone wants happiness out of life. God wants everyone to be happy. Then why are so many lacking in this area? One might expect poor people—who have little of this world's goods—not to have it, yet many of them do. One might expect people who have everything money can buy to possess happiness, but many of them don't.

Shouldn't those who are beautifully formed and physically attractive have it? If people are adequately talented, especially with ability in sports, and can command millions of dollars in contracts, and have countless accolades heaped upon them, shouldn't they be happy? We all know of people in these categories who are most unhappy. What is the recipe for happiness? What is the main ingredient?

One of the biggest causes for a deficit in this area for many people is that they seek happiness for its own sake. It cannot be found that way. Happiness cannot be an end or a goal. It is not a destination.

Happiness Depends on Relationship

To study how God planned for us to obtain happiness, let us first ask, on what does true happiness depend? It is not built on popularity, status, geography, or money. In brief, maximum happiness depends most heavily on one thing: relationship. It is a by-product of that and that alone. In the focus of this book, it is a law-guided relationship based on a covenant made with God, first and foremost. There is a sense in which we never "find" happiness by seeking it. But by seeking God, happiness finds us.

The seventeenth-century French mathematician and philosopher, Blaise Pascal, once noted, "Happiness is neither within us only or without us; it is the union of ourselves with God."

This "union of ourselves with God" depends on our constantly accepting His truth as presented in His Word and continually exercising the wisdom of that truth in our lives. If this is not done, life will deteriorate and decline, and happiness will become ever more elusive.

The best condensation of God's truth, His recipe for happiness, is found in the Ten Commandments. But let's first look at why everyone needs such a small list of "do's and don'ts."

The Fall and Its Results

By simply observing society, whether by reading literature, newspapers and magazines, watching television, or listening to the radio, it is not difficult to see that "all have sinned and fall short of the glory of God" (Romans 3:23). It is as equally discernible that everyone has sinned because everyone was born with a sinful heart. Everyone was born with a sinful heart because the parents of the human family sinned in the Garden of Eden.

There are, of course, numerous individuals who affirm that the stories of Genesis, including the Fall, are pure myth. They will admit that at the heart of this "tale" there may be a core of truth from which it has been woven. They think the "Garden of Eden" story is simply the end result of people trying to understand and explain the dilemma of life in which they have found themselves.

To hold such a view is to have no answer, then, for no person born has ever had to be trained how to be bad. Since creation, no mother has ever had to say to her little boy, "Kick your sister! Pull her hair! Get mad and sass me!" Nor has a father counseled his daughter, "Stick your tongue out at your brother! Spit on him! Have a temper tantrum! You're too angelic!"

These actions are so often automatic and children instead have to be trained how to be good. Bad actions just come naturally. Since the heart is evil, it will ultimately boil out, spill over, and stain anyone nearby. This is why it becomes so necessary for parents to set limits (or give laws) early, so as to direct children toward a disciplined life.

The Way It All Began

Though there are those who think some elements of the Genesis account of the Fall are too bizarre, Genesis does explain what happened. If we concentrate less on the details and more on the substance of the elements, the picture becomes significantly clearer and loses some of its strange elements.

First, let us consider why Satan chose to embody a serpent to tempt Eve. There had to have been many other possibilities. Why not a dog or a cat? This would seem more logical.

Though little is given about it in the Bible, there was unquestionably an early enchantment with snakes. In almost every pagan worship center that has come to light as a result of archaeological excavations, a fascination with serpents is evident. Personally, I have seen them on fertility plaques, carved into altars, painted on pottery, formed into jar handles, and entwined around cult stands.

At Beersheba a few years ago, our archaeological team discovered the only horned sacrificial altar that has been found so far. It was exactly the dimensions of an altar described in the Bible, five cubits by five cubits by three cubits (Exodus 38:1). It had been dismantled and the stones reused for the construction of a wall during the time of King Hezekiah, who ruled from 729 B.C.

Since Hezekiah was such a good king, and since the celebration of the Passover in Jerusalem helped to bring about a great revival, we wondered why he had allowed, perhaps even ordered, this altar to be demolished in favor of the need for a simple wall. When the unique stones of the altar were reconstructed, we noticed that on one side of a cornerstone, two snakes had been carved. It seems obvious that the altar had been paganized and for this reason it had to be destroyed.

Who knows, but perhaps all this fascination with snakes finds its origin in the Garden of Eden incident.

After choosing to embody a serpent, Satan singled out Eve to tempt. Why? It was for at least two reasons. First, she did not receive the command directly from God; she got it from Adam. Receiving something secondhand is not as strong as it is if received firsthand. And second, since Eve was a woman, perhaps she possessed a little more creative ingenuity and a bit more speculative intuition. Satan thought she was an easier prey.

It would appear that the "tree of the knowledge of good and evil" was not unlike other trees of the same family. However, it is certain it was not an apple tree, for apples cannot grow in the Tigris-Euphrates valley area, the place where the Bible identifies the location of the Garden of Eden. It was the interpretation of medieval artists that gave rise to the apple being involved, which has caused it, even until today, to be the universal sign of temptation, especially one with a bite out of the side.

If the tree was not an apple tree, what kind was it? While it really makes no difference, it would be likely that it was a date palm, or a fig tree. In any case God simply chose to use that particular tree as a test of obedience for Eve. It was to determine if Eve would follow God's instructions (His laws) or do her own thing. Eve could have ingested fruit from another tree that looked and tasted the same, and there would have been no ill effect. It is clear from the text that the fruit on that one tree was not poisonous to the body. But eating of it against God's order would cause an inner, spiritual explosion to occur.

Understanding Sin

The divine-human partnership that began in the Garden is immediately seen as having a higher intimacy than the divine-animal relationship.

God made animals to act according to instinct. In a sense they were preprogrammed to "do their thing." But Adam and Eve were created with God breathing into them a life after making them in His own "image and likeness" (Genesis 1:26-27). This gave them a "personality" with its accompanying "free choice." God could have made them more marionette-like with invisible strings coming down out of heaven, directing every action and word. But such an existence would have been stilted, artificial, and affected.

God did not want shallow devotion that could only have come from a robotic existence. He knew He was losing the allegiance of many who would opt for the "wide gate" in order to have a few who would choose to enter the "narrow gate." But He wanted a relationship that would lift people higher than any animal could reach. So God allowed human beings to have a choice. As a result, sin began by a willful disobedience to a clearly given and plainly understood command of God.

Satan, mad at God, determined to "get even" for his dismissal from the heavenly court. He wanted to get back at God where it would hurt Him most— His gift of free will for humankind. He had to drive a wedge into the intimacy that existed. He could only accomplish his desire by deception and solicitation. He had to stir doubt in the minds of Eve and Adam by making them think God was more interested in himself than He was in them. Satan wanted them to think they could have what they were being denied by simply taking it, even though in so doing they would be directly disobeying God.

An Obedience Test

Following God's dictum, Eve at first seems to have ignored the tree, considering it off bounds and not suitable for food. Trusting God's restrictions to be right, it never bothered her as to why it was taboo.

But now, as a result of Satan's suggestive, but evil, logic, Eve looked at the tree for the first time, interestedly. His argument followed this line: "Do you know why God doesn't want you to eat from that tree? Not because He cares about you! But because it will be bad for Him! He's not looking out for you. He's selfishly considering what is best for Him, looking out for himself. Everyone has to do that; you might as well do it too."

Such a rationale could not be further from the truth. God has no agenda to protect His interests. Being all-powerful, He needs none. His total focus is what is best for us. His laws are not fences to hold us in but to keep evil away.

When we take our trust from God, thinking for the slightest moment that when God speaks or acts He does not have our best interest at heart, we open ourselves up to all kinds of twists of logic that only lead away from the truth. The moment Eve began to take her trust from God, she then looked at the fruit of the tree with different eyes.

Eve saw that the fruit was "beautiful to look at," would be "good to the taste," and would make her "wise" (Genesis 3:6). As she looked, in reality, she saw the beautiful, the good, and the true. She thought to herself, "There it is! All I really want out of life. Why is God keeping it from me? I guess Satan was right. God must care more about himself than He cares about me. Why should I not taste of it? What can be wrong with the beautiful, the good, and the true?"

When Eve flippantly took her trust away from God, a result of having given ear to the evil counsel of Satan, it became easier for her not to believe what God had told her. This was so because distrust always breeds disbelief. "If I can't trust God, then I can't believe what He says," she reasoned.

The place where every Christian must begin the odyssey of faith is, "God has my best interest at heart. I know because He says so in His Word. Therefore, I can trust all of His commands."

At the time one harbors for the slightest moment the idea that "God has designed laws to withhold something from me that I want, even what I deserve," he has stepped away from the path of faith. At the point where he thinks, "God cares more about himself than He does about me," he has turned from the high road of trust to the low road that leads to distrust, to disbelief, and finally to disaster.

Sin's Two Methods of Operation

All sin begins with disobedience to what God has said to do or not to do. It is a violation of His instruction. It can happen in two main ways.

Sin is first a premature taking of something before we are ready for it.

I recall incidents from my childhood when, sometimes at 3:00 in the afternoon, I would ask Mother for a candy bar. The answer was always, "No, it will spoil your dinner." I never could understand that logic. How could a candy bar make my food spoil? It would taste the same no matter when I ate it! I couldn't see that the candy bar taken before mealtime would have a dramatic effect on my appetite.

Mother was not denying me the candy bar because it was bad food. She would often say, "You may have it after you have eaten your meal, but not before." She knew that the quality of the candy bar and the quality of the food at the meal would not be affected with the eating or not eating of the candy at that particular time. But she also knew that my desire for more nourishing food would diminish and such a practice continued would be injurious to my health.

Mother was not denying my request out of her own best interest, but out of mine. She knew that I would be the one hurt and her denial, we might term it "her law," was borne of what she knew would be best for me.

It would seem that if Eve had kept her trust in God and had not listened to Satan's skewed reasoning, the day would have come when the LORD would have said to her, "Now Eve, by following my instructions, you are ready for the fruit. Go eat all of it you want. Obedience has prepared you in such a way that the fruit now will not hurt you; it will rather help you. Eat to your heart's delight."

Eve was not ready for the food of that tree at the point of the temptation because she was about to take it in disobedience. This was the reason for God's denial of it at that particular time. She would only be ready for the fruit when she would no longer have to take it in violation of God's command.

There is a world of difference between our taking something and something taking us, a great chasm between our having something and something having us, or our owning something and something owning us. In each case the former is desired; the latter is always to be shunned. God always seeks to prevent such from happening. It occurs when the legitimate assumes illegitimate control, or when what was intended by God to serve us instead becomes our master.

Since sin is always so pervasive, so cunning, so deceptive, and so subtle, we may not know the point at which such a change starts to occur. God does. His moral laws are designed to protect us from passing that line; we must always defer to His knowledge.

Sin is also a misuse of something God intended for good purpose.

This was not Eve's problem at the point of her sin. This is usually the next step away from God after we have disobeyed Him for what to us at the moment seemed the right time to use legitimate things.

Everything God has given has a good purpose. It was with this in mind that He gave it to us. But it is always possible to misuse, misapply, or misappropriate the gift by putting it to a purpose never intended by God. To give a specific illustration, God never intended for tobacco to be inhaled or absorbed into our bodies. Unquestionably it is because it is so addictive, and in the long run, injurious to our health.

Then one might ask, "If God knew it would be detrimental, why did He make it available to us?" Maybe it is because it is one of the best moth repellents around. It probably cannot be used for that purpose today lest the user, by the odor accompanying him, be assumed to be a smoker. If the modern tobacco industry would spend some of its profit on research to determine what other good purposes their product could viably serve, there would likely be dozens of other areas where it would be of benefit.

A case can be made that God did not intend alcohol to be ingested for it dulls sensitivity, slows reaction time, makes one less responsible, and more apt to commit other sins. If four beers makes one drunk and out of control, then one beer makes one one-fourth drunk and one-fourth out of control. If alcohol today were given the stringent tests required of any other drug before it could be approved for consumption, it would fail miserably on every level.

What was God's purpose for making it available to us? It seems likely that it was for the purpose of preservation and disinfection. Consumed in the human body it does little of either.

It is then *most important* to realize that God is most concerned about what is best for us. This being so, it follows then that we too should be most interested in what is best for us. Anything that erodes, effaces, or destroys the priceless thing called personality, God opposes. Neither does He approve of anything that makes us lose control. Whatever God opposes is sin, no matter whether it is taking something before we are ready for it or a misuse of something God intended for a good purpose.

Eve was most fascinated by what she presumed she was missing out on at that present moment. God's instruction had more of the future effect in mind than it did the present denied pleasure. The sinner gives less and less regard to what will happen tomorrow as a result of what he is doing today. His philosophy is quite simply, "Eat, drink and be merry, for tomorrow we die."

Then properly considered, the sinner often mortgages his future by spending tomorrow's assets today. In contrast, by biblical direction, the Christian is told not to damage the future in any way by what is done today. So in comparison to the sinner, the Christian, by living a disciplined life, following biblical principles, and making some sacrifices, invests each day into tomorrow. He is able, then, to watch each tomorrow grow bigger with more options, more opportunities, and more happiness. In short, the sinner's tomorrow shrinks; the Christian's tomorrow expands. In the end, of the two, the Christian is happier.

Horace Mann, an American educator of nearly two centuries ago, once wrote, "In vain do they talk of happiness who never subdued an impulse in obedience to a principle. He who never sacrificed a present to a future good, or a personal to a general one, can speak of happiness only as the blind do of colors."

God's Solution: Laws to Live By

When God created the human family, His "dilemma" was, "How can I help people not to take good things before they are ready for them? How can I *make* people not misuse good things by making them serve the wrong purposes? How can I *make* people more selfless, more mindful of others, more giving in their lifestyle? How can I *make* them have a higher self-image until they see themselves as living on too high a level of life to allow themselves to sin?"

God needed a way that would stop the downward pull of sin's whirlpool, and reverse the downward slide of self-respect. He had to have a way of not only forgiving the sin committed, but also of providing a way to minimize its effect on the sinner. In the Old Testament He did this by instituting a set of laws to live by.

God wanted these laws to be succinctly stated, but yet to be all encompassing. He wanted them to cover both people's responsibility to themselves and their responsibility to others. He wanted these commandments to be strong enough to show all people the effects that the Fall had on them. He wanted them to see how helpless they were in trying to live up to the standard these laws required. He wanted all people to see the evil cores they had inside themselves which often made them their own worst enemies. He wanted to show everyone how much they needed what only He could give—forgiveness and cleansing.

The Old Testament Solution: A Sacrifice

After Adam and Eve sinned, and as long as time will last, forgiveness will always be our greatest need. The forgiveness that is needed could only come about through the death of something or someone innocent, who would be willing to bear our punishment.

At first this was done by the sacrifice of an animal, which because of its innocence and by means of this sacrifice, could atone for the sins of the guilty party. Only innocent blood could atone for the guilt of sin. We do not know when this began, but there is a suggestion that it occurred right after Adam and Eve sinned. We are told in Genesis 3:21 that God clothed them in the skins of animals. This implies the death of animals to meet the need of every human.

Noah practiced the sacrifice of animals as soon as he exited the ark (Genesis 8:20). But did people in time completely lose all their connections to the LORD?

While this may not be affirmed with certainty, it is clear from what Joshua said in his farewell speech to the people of Israel that Abraham didn't learn about God from his father and mother. He was reared in an idol-worshiping home (Joshua 24:2). After he moved to Canaan, it is also clear that whatever had caused Abraham to come to God and abandon the idolatry of his upbringing, he wanted everyone to know that he did not trust in idols, as did all the people of the land. He built altars to the LORD at every stopping place in testimony to his faith in God (Genesis 12:7-8; 13:4, 18).

Soon after Lot had been freed from his captors, Abraham was somewhat disappointed that his nephew had chosen to return to Sodom instead of staying with him. The LORD then instructed Abraham to take several three-year-old animals and birds (Genesis 15:8-9), all of which were later specified in the law to be used for sacrificial animals, and cut them in half. Later the same night, the LORD made a covenant with Abraham to give the land of Canaan to his descendants. These animals played a part in that covenant God was establishing with Abraham.

Was this all possibly symbolic of the One who was to come? Was atonement somehow involved? We are not told, but in the same context Abraham is told of the eventual coming of his descendants to the land of Canaan (Genesis 15:16). Redemption from bondage is prefigured here, for it took a Paschal Lamb's blood to make it possible.

It would seem that Abraham was being schooled in God's grand design for the whole human race. But this "Father of the Faith" had to be schooled in trust because he had little if any training and background in following God. Yet it must be understood that while it was necessary for Abraham to grow *in* faith, he could not grow *into* faith. Faith produces results at the point of confession and instantaneous conversion results.

In Abraham's day sacrifices were being done at altars, but they were made mainly to placate the anger of gods who were thought to lose their tempers for one reason or another. When the people became most desperate, they would sacrifice their own children to their deity.

Abraham needed to learn that there is a right kind of sacrifice to be made, and there is also a wrong kind. Innocent animals are acceptable, even desired, but not innocent children. Later God made this clear to Moses in the law given on Sinai (Leviticus 10:1-5). But being so new to the faith, Abraham had to be given the truth in a way more suitable to his own personal need.

It seems certain that Abraham would have gone through with the sacrifice of Isaac if the LORD had not provided a substitute. But the substitute was provided, and it was a ram, the very animal later specified to atone for a sinner who had committed willful sins (Leviticus 5:14-16).

Was not God also giving to Abraham, and to all the world through the Scripture, a picture in prophecy of what was to come? In the mind of Abraham his only son was already "dead" as he made the three-day journey it would have taken to get from Hebron to Mt. Moriah. There was a sacrifice, a substitutionary one. It all occurred where centuries later pavements would run red with the blood of innocent animals to atone for the sins of the guilty. God knew this was all going to have its final punctuation with the once-for-all shedding of the blood of His Son, Jesus Christ, near the same spot.

There is a greater lesson in this situation with Abraham, for him and for us as well. It was a lesson that life is meaningless without love—a love that is properly focused on One who is the embodiment of perfect love. A love-generated plan of redemption through a sacrifice was not an afterthought or a simple adjustment after the Fall. It was not Plan B after Plan A had failed. God had written this lesson plan long before the creation of the world (Ephesians 1:4-10).

God could have made people robots and preprogrammed them to want only Him. But love would not allow God to make us without allowing alternative choices to himself. God knew we would sin, so He planned that His unlimited love would be presented as an option. It was one that would hopefully elicit a similar love in response. The kind of love God would receive was important to Him.

In Abraham's situation, God was helping him clarify the kind of love he had for his Maker in comparison to the kind of love he had for Isaac. In effect, God was saying to Abraham, "This test is designed to help you know if you love Me because of what I have done for you, or if you love Me because of Who I am."

Why was this so crucial to Abraham? If his love was based on God's performance alone, it would weaken when at some point God would not perform the way Abraham expected. If Abraham's love was based on God as a Person, the love would hold strong regardless of God's acts.

To illustrate, any marriage that is based on performance, such as cleaning the house, cooking, earning a decent living, or whatever else might be "done," would not last through times of illness or other incapacity to perform. A love that is person-based will grow even stronger when there is an inability to perform expected duties because it is based on who the person is intrinsically and not on what actions one can do.

Why such a lesson at this time? God knew His plan to give His Son in love to become a human being would soon be necessary to fulfill the law. He wanted to show what kind of love response would be required. No matter how perfect the law was, it could only be fulfilled in Christ.

Until then, His laws were given to maintain civil order, ensure proper ceremonial procedures, promote good health practices, and foster good morality.

Understanding II Biblical Law

We concluded the lesson in the last chapter by talking about the Old Testament sacrificial system. It required the blood of innocent animals to cover the sins of guilty sinners. The system had to suffice, as imperfect as it was, until God's "fulness of the time" (Galatians 4:4 KJV) came. Then He could send Jesus to fulfill that plan.

Changeable Laws

Until Jesus came, God relied on a system of laws to maintain civil order, ensure proper ceremonial procedures, promote good health practices, and foster good morality. The laws governing the first three of these categories—civil, ceremonial, and health—would necessarily have to be applied in a temporary way to meet the needs of the specific situations that existed at that time. What would be injurious to health then would not be so in later times. What laws may have been required for orderly ceremonies then would necessarily change if the ceremonial practices changed. The same could be said for civil laws.

To illustrate, today we have a civil law that allows for a right turn on a red light at an intersection after a stop, if no traffic is oncoming. Such a law would have been useless then with few intersections and no red lights. A law in Old Testament times that would limit speed to 55 miles per hour would also have been meaningless, since camels and donkeys could not go quite that fast!

This should help us understand why there seems to be some very strange laws in the Old Testament that, for the most part, are now archaic. No one today is expected to follow them, though some very orthodox Jews may.

Archaic Old Testament Laws

Here are some examples: "When you build a new house, make a parapet around your roof, so that you may not bring guilt of bloodshed on your house if someone falls from the roof" (Deuteronomy 22:8).

People at that time built small houses with rooms as small as six by ten feet. Their roofs were flat. In time, these became conveniently usable as extensions to their living quarters, accessed by a simple ladder or stairs constructed on the inside or the outside. The reason for using the roof was not alone to provide more space. At certain times of the day it was cooler there.

We can tell much about such houses from the description given of the house in Jericho where the Moabite king, Eglon, had his local headquarters. It was there where Eglon received the judge Ehud, who was bringing him the tribute payment the Moabite enemy had forced on the Hebrews. This house had not only a "private chamber" on the roof, but it also had toilet facilities available to the king. We know this to be so since Ehud had time to escape only because the king's bodyguards assumed the king was "covering his feet"—the Hebrew way of saying, they thought he was "in the restroom" (Judges 3:20-25).

This law concerning the parapet was meant to make the owner take more responsibility concerning the safety of guests, who might be visiting "upstairs" and accidentally fall from the roof if no wall surrounded it. Almost no one today would think of building a house with a flat roof containing living quarters, so the law is ignored. That in no way means that people today can be negligent concerning the safety of others. The designs have changed, but we still have laws to ensure the safety of other people.

Deuteronomy 22:10 orders farmers not to "plow with an ox and a donkey yoked together." Besides the fact that nearly all farmers use tractors today and would not even consider using such animals, the Bible was concerned about cruelty to animals. It would be most difficult for these two animals to work together.

Consider also Deuteronomy 22:11: "Do not wear clothes of wool and linen woven together." Is there anyone today who would insist that any garment of mixed types of thread should not be worn by Christians? It is highly unlikely. Clothes blended with Dacron and cotton wear longer and wrinkle far less than material that is made of only cotton.

We need to ask though, why was such a law important at that time? It seems probable that in numerous ways there was always a great danger of God's people copying the evil habits and practices of the pagan Canaanites. It may well be presumed that in the minds of these people such garments were directly associated with their religious ideas of fertility and sexual immorality, thus God opposed the use of such combinations in materials.

Consider the law of Deuteronomy 22:12, where "tassels" were required "on the four corners of the cloak you wear." No one except "letter-of-the-law" Jews requires this today.

God was also very concerned about the maintenance of health in Old Testament times. Pork was forbidden as a meat for consumption, not because it was bad for every follower of God, but because it was *bad at that time*. It did not come from an animal that met both the required "split hoof" and "cud chewing" requirement (Deuteronomy 14:6-8). Why is it then that bacon, ham, and pork are eaten by most Christians today and they do not consider it wrong or injurious to their health?

Moreover, though rabbit meat is one of the best meats that can be consumed today (it is very low in cholesterol), it was forbidden in the law (Deuteronomy 14:7). A rabbit chewed a cud but did not have split hooves. One may wonder why God would consider the feet and the chewing habits of animals important considerations in the consumption of flesh.

While pork is a healthy meat to eat, if poorly cooked or badly preserved, it is indeed unwise to ingest. It can cause trichinosis, a deadly food poison. Also, without refrigeration it is unsafe for human consumption. If rabbit meat is consumed before a frost, it carries a deadly germ that causes tularemia, more commonly known as "rabbit fever." In Bible lands, where it so seldom frosts, it is never wise to eat the meat of a rabbit.

Unchangeable Moral Laws

The moral laws in the Old Testament *do not change*. They are as essential to contentment and fulfillment today as they were then.

These laws should be looked at in the same way one views the laws of nature. As an example, consider the law of gravity. No one would think of saying, "This law is a nineteenth-century law. I now live in the twenty-first century. The law of gravity is an old law. I don't need to obey it. I'll just climb this tall building and jump down to prove that this law does not apply to me."

Whatever the rationale used by that person, if he jumps he will not bounce when he hits the ground. He will splatter! He will not break the law of gravity. He will break himself against the law of gravity! So too, we do not break the moral law; we only break ourselves against it, to our own detriment.

These moral laws, summed up in the Ten Commandments, cannot be open to individual interpretation and application. No one must be allowed to step up to God's counter and say, "Now I will obey this law, but that one doesn't apply to me. I'll disregard it." They were, and are, all to be regarded and observed in the last age, in this age, or in any age if people are to happily maximize their own God-given potential.

Casuistic or Case Laws

Up to the present time, at least eight law codes that applied to different peoples in times past have come to light in whole or in part through archaeological discoveries. Some of them are very fragmentary; others are more complete. It is clear that all of them have laws stated in a similar fashion. The legislation that proved to be most effective was called casuistic law, sometimes referred to as case law.

This type of law is stated in the third person singular. It begins with an "if," showing that it is conditional, and is very specific concerning the infraction to which it is aimed. Then there always follows the punishment that is to be administered to the violator. Many of the laws of the Bible are stated in this way. Sometimes it is the most effective way to express a law because the civil punishment can be delineated quite clearly.

The set of laws most often compared to biblical law is the Code of Hammurabi, a king of the early Babylonian kingdom who ruled from 1792–1750 B.C. There is great similarity between the two, but in general the biblical laws are more merciful, more liberal, and more considerate of equal justice. Exceptions are when an action taken will damage the priceless, personal, and God-given asset of "personality," or when the invaluable structure of the "family" is threatened. In these instances, biblical law is usually harsher.

In both cases, however, laws were often more strict than is the case in our day. The reason for this is that society was far more primitive and elementary. It lacked in development, maturity, and sophistication, and laws accordingly had to be more exact and more threatening. It was somewhat similar to the relationship of a parent to a child. Instructions are far more frequently given and specifically defined for nearly everything when the child is small compared to when he is older and has learned more. There are many more "don'ts" given at the early stage of life than there are when the child is older and understands far more.

To illustrate, in Hammurabi's Code, the very first law stated is, "If a citizen has accused a citizen and has indicted him for a murder and has not substantiated the charge, his accuser shall be put to death." Since society then was based far more on oral statements alone, the danger of falsely accusing someone, as children might do today to escape punishment or to "get even," was much more serious. As a result, the punishment needed to be more severe to keep people honest. Because of the severity of the law, it is doubtful that very many people made false accusations that could not be proven.

Apodictic Laws

To show the more advanced position of the Bible, and its more advanced enlightenment, the law given for a similar infraction was stated in what is called an apodictic manner, with no punishment being delineated. Exodus 23:7 simply stated, "Have nothing to do with a false charge; and do not put an innocent or honest person to death, for I will not acquit the guilty."

Notice that in this type of law, the tense is in the more direct second person singular ("You shall not!"). It is far more inclusive, and has the sense of,

"Don't you ever, under any circumstance, for any reason, at any place, or at any time do thus and so." Never is there a punishment stated to tell what will occur if the command is violated. This type of law is only found in the Bible. It is the unique contribution of God's Word to society. The only place in history where something similar is found is in a treaty drawn up by a victor over his vanquished enemy, wherein is stated a set of limits, such as, "You shall do this, and this, and this. You shall not do this, and this, and this."

Trial by ordeal.

Again Hammurabi's Code states, "If a citizen has indicted a citizen for sorcery and does not substantiate the charge, the one who is indicted for sorcery shall go to the river and shall throw himself in. If the river overwhelms him, [then] his indicter shall take away his house. If the river exculpates that citizen and he is preserved, the one who indicted him for sorcery shall die, [and] the one who threw himself into the river shall take away his house."

What is described here is a law where the punishment prescribed is a "trial by ordeal." The guilt or innocence is decided by the ordeal of being thrown into the Euphrates river, apparently with hands tied. If the accused drowned, he was guilty; if he lived, he was considered innocent, and he was then compensated for his ordeal by being awarded the property of the one who falsely accused him.

There is indeed a law covering a similar situation in the Bible, but it is far more advanced than such a primitive treatment of the accused. It is found in Deuteronomy 19:15. "One witness is not enough to convict a man accused of any crime or offense he may have committed. A matter must be established by the testimony of two or three witnesses."

Though this apodictic law is not stated in the normal second person singular, it has the same force, and again no punishment is delineated. In His justice, the LORD recognized the need for witnesses to establish the guilt of an individual.

There is one law mentioned in the Bible that some have labeled "trial by ordeal," but to this writer it is labeled somewhat incorrectly. It is found in Numbers 5:11-31. It involves a situation where there would likely be no witnesses. A husband suspects his wife is guilty of adultery. He is to bring her before the priest, who then brings her "before the LORD" (v. 16). She must endure a procedure which in that day would have made anyone guilty readily confess or act in such a way as to belie the guilt.

It should be emphasized that in this situation the one accused is "innocent until proven guilty," as opposed to the person in the Hammurabi Code where the one accused is "guilty until proven innocent."

In such situations in that day, a guilty person was more likely to be discovered by such a procedure than would be the case today. They were not as sophisticated, not as cagey, not as experienced, and therefore more susceptible to being caught in that kind of ordeal.

This story should prove the point. Some years ago a teacher of a first grade class was aware of a student having taken an item from another, but she did not know for sure who was guilty. After endeavoring unsuccessfully to gain a confession, she came upon an idea of how to make the thief reveal his own identity.

Before she sent the children to the lunch room, she told them she was going to prepare a test that they would have to take when they returned, one that she believed would determine who was guilty. While they were away, she turned a galvanized wash tub upside down and placed it in the long narrow cloakroom adjacent to the classroom. There were no windows in the room, but there were entrance and exit doors that provided adequate illumination. She turned off the overhead light. On the top of the tub she spread lamp black, which in the dim light could not be detected by the children.

When the children returned, the guilty one having had plenty of time to consider his theft and worry about the test, the teacher informed them of the tub. She then told each child to enter the room alone, one at a time. While in the room, each was to think about whether or not he or she was guilty, then touch the top of the tub with the palm of the hand.

After all had gone through the room, the teacher then told all students to hold up the hands that had touched the tub. When they raised them, they were all black but one. The guilty student had thought to himself, "She said she would find out who was guilty by this test. I'll fool her. I won't touch the tub." His guilt caused him to get caught.

Such a test would probably not work with adults today, but with the childish knowledge and demeanor of adults in that day, the ordeal of the one accused being thrown in the river caused the guilty person to be revealed. He likely didn't even try to survive, knowing he was guilty. He felt himself trapped in the ordeal.

Marriage, adultery, and the family.

The sin of adultery was, and always will be, destructive to the family institution. It always damages the mental, physical, and psychological health of the husband, wife, and children who make up the family. The biblical law was intended to protect both husband and wife from destroying the unit upon which their future contentment depended. In Hammurabi's Code there seems to have been little concern about adultery.

It is noteworthy that the Hammurabi Code also gave more emphasis to economic considerations than does the Bible. For example, consider these laws:

"If a citizen has been carried away captive, and there is sustenance in his house, his wife . . . shall guard her property and shall not enter the household of another. If that wife does not guard her property but enters into the household of another, they shall convict his wife and cast her into the water. [But] if a citizen has been carried away captive, and there is no sustenance in his house, his wife may enter into another household, and no crime may be imputed to this woman."

Biblical law was far more considerate of the people in similar situations, though it did not give nearly as much regard to economic considerations. In the case of a recently married couple, God did not want the newlyweds to jeopardize their contentment in the event of war. Notice: "If a man is recently married, he must not be sent to war or have any other duty laid on him. For one year he is to be free to stay at home and bring contentment to the wife he has married" (Deuteronomy 24:5).

In the case of children being submissive to their parents, the Hammurabi Code was severe. It stated, "If a son has struck his father, they shall cut off his hand." But, recognizing the threat disobedient children would be in the future to themselves, as well as to society, the biblical law was even more severe. It states, "Anyone who attacks his father or his mother must be put to death" (Exodus 21:15). It seems highly unlikely that there were very many children going about with one hand amputated, nor were there many if any who would smite a parent. Both laws were serious enough to prevent the infraction.

Milk and meat consumption.

One of the laws in the Old Testament most difficult to understand is found in three places, which emphasizes its importance to the Israelites. It is found in Exodus 23:19; 34:26; and again in Deuteronomy 14:21. It is given in the apodictic form. "Do not cook a young goat in its mother's milk."

In not one of the three incidents is found a context that gives the slightest hint as to why such an act was considered wrong. For centuries, Jews have interpreted the injunction to mean that no meat or meat product should be eaten together with any milk or milk product at any one meal. Even today, especially in Israel whether one is a Jew or not, it is not possible to eat the two together in a kosher restaurant. Separate dishes, silverware, pots, and pans are to be used for the different diets. Even in the kitchens will be found separate sinks to wash the dishes of the two diets. Most hotels have different dining rooms used to serve the foods of the different diets.

Is that what the Lord intended? Jesus was speaking against such practices when He said, "Nothing outside a man can make him 'unclean' by going into him. Rather, it is what comes out of a man that makes him 'unclean'" (Mark 7:16).

The problem solved.

The information that emerged as a result of a Syrian farmer plowing his field in 1928 led me to a theory as to why this law was considered so important as to have it recorded in three places in the Old Testament. His plow happened to catch on a flagstone under the soil. After several attempts to reset his plow so his ox could pull through the spot, he upended the stone. It opened a subterranean passageway to an underground tomb.

The farmer found the tomb to contain some valuable pottery, which he knew he could turn into cash. He took it to the nearest antique market and sold it. Ultimately, all of this came to the attention of the director of the Antiquities Department of the country. Later, when some archaeological work was done on the site, it was determined to be an early Greek tomb. Enough information emerged to indicate a long lost city, named Ugarit, had to be nearby.

Archaeological work was begun on a mound not far from the tomb, and after several seasons of digging, it was determined the long lost city of Ugarit had at last been found. Numerous clay tablets were unearthed on which poetry was written about Baal, the god of the ancient Canaanites.

In one poem entitled, "The Birth of the Great and Beautiful God," two lines are found which read, "Mix a kid in milk, blend a goat in butter." This was an edict in direct opposition to the prohibition found in the Bible. It is now thought to have been related to a "magical milk charm" practiced by these pagan people. It was a practice in which they killed an offspring of a mother goat, and after blending it with its mother's milk, offered it to Baal as an inducement to fertility. The food was then eaten by the "worshipers," completing the pagan ritual.

It seems likely that the LORD wanted to spare the Israelites from an easy slide into idolatry by prohibiting a food regimen that, while otherwise safe, led to evil practices in the Canaanite culture of the time.

Why laws with no punishments are given.

A question that needs to be asked is, why are apodictic laws only found in the Bible? And why is there never a punishment stated?

It is my contention that such a type of law was given in instances where the punishment that ensues is the automatic end result of the sin itself. In other words, the sin has the punishment built within it. It is automatic. It is like the rubber ball on the end of the elastic line. When it is batted away, it returns just as quickly to strike the one who first hit it away.

Numerous scriptures in the Bible verify this end result of certain sinful actions on the part of people. Here are a few.

"But whoever fails to find me harms himself" (Proverbs 8:36).

"Your own conduct and actions have brought this upon you" (Jeremiah 4:18).

"Your wickedness will punish you; your backsliding will rebuke you" (Jeremiah 2:19).

"For the waywardness of the simple will kill them, and the complacency of fools will destroy them" (Proverbs 1:32).

"But am I the one they are provoking? declares the LORD. Are they not rather harming themselves, to their own shame?" (Jeremiah 7:19).

"The look on their faces testifies against them; they parade their sin like Sodom; they do not hide it. Woe to them! They have brought disaster upon themselves" (Isaiah 3:9).

There are certain sins one can do that may affect only himself, for which, especially in a free society, he cannot be punished by the legal authorities. In Old Testament times, when everyone lived in such close proximity, and when the responsibility for how one's actions affected the entire community, laws had to be more strict and more rigidly enforced.

An example would be in the case of homosexuality. It could not be allowed by anyone, even with what is termed today "consenting adults." A death penalty was mandatory. Few today would advocate that such a sin should be punished by surrendering one's life.

However, the emotional damage, the personality scars, the anti-family end result, as well as the numerous kinds of sexually transmitted diseases—such as herpes, chlamydia, syphilis, gonorrhea, and more recently AIDS—all are built-in punishments for the sin committed. If society would live by the Ten Commandments, especially the seventh one, these "built-in" punishments would disappear in one or two generations.

Were these diseases known in Old Testament times? The answer is most emphatically "Yes!" With the wide open, promiscuous, and unbridled immoral sexual practices, even sex with animals, the incidences of plagues of epidemic proportions were always present. But with no modern names to label the different infections, they were lumped into the broad category of "leprosy."

Could this not be the clear reason why sometimes the Israelites were given the command, as to Joshua at Jericho, and to Saul with respect to the Amalekites, not to spare any man, woman, child, animal, or garment among the enemy? It was not that God was cruel in the Old Testament, but rather it was the only way to save society from committing a type of personal suicide by engaging in immorality. More will be said about this in chapter nine.

CHAPTER III
The First Commandment

Have no other gods before me (Exodus 20:3).

These unique laws we call the Ten Commandments are found in two places in the Old Testament: Exodus 20:1-17 and Deuteronomy 5:1-22. Moses was given the whole law, the *Torah*, on Mount Sinai, and that *Torah* is summed up in these commandments.

There seems to be no special sacredness about the number ten, although Hebrew (like most languages) counted from base ten, probably because of ten fingers. The institution of the tithe (Genesis 28:22) shows how this basis of ten could take on a religious meaning.

In Exodus 20:1, **All these words** are intentionally connected to the word **spoke**. The source, God, is the main stress, followed by the purpose, to keep them from returning to slavery (v. 2). Then follows the content, the ten rules (vv. 3-17).

Not being a God of speculation, the LORD expressed these ten basic guidelines in terms of moral imperatives, not in philosophical terms. He is a God of history in that He had brought the people out of slavery. He was giving these ten principles to enable them to keep from returning to slavery.

In the past thirty years I have had thousands of college freshmen taking my introductory class in Old Testament. I ask them to rearrange the commandments, putting what seemed to them to be the most important laws first. About 90% of the time the order will be arranged as follows:

1. No murder (6)
2. No stealing (8)
3. No lying (9)
4. No immorality (7)
5. Honor parents (5)
6. No coveting (10)
7. No images (2)
8. No other gods (1)
9. No name in vain (4)
10. Remember the Sabbath Day (3)

Murder is nearly always considered the number one sin to avoid. It has been striking to me to observe that people tend to think that avoiding the sins against other people is more important than avoiding the sins against God. Few realize that if a proper relationship with God is considered primary, one will not have to worry about any of the other sins, for one cannot maintain a right relationship with people without a right relationship with God.

How differently from my students did Christ look at the order. He told the rich young ruler the first and greatest commandment is, "Love the LORD your God with all your heart and with all your soul and with all your strength and with all your mind" (Luke 10:27). This is simply a paraphrase of this first commandment. Then Jesus followed with the responsibility one must have to society, "Love your neighbor as yourself."

Let us note what this first commandment does not say, "You shall have no other gods except me, or other than me." While the phrase in the Hebrew *al panai* is not easy to translate, it does mean either "before me," or "in addition to me." It is not because exclusiveness cannot be expressed in Hebrew, for we have it in Isaiah 45:6, "There is none besides me. I am the LORD, and there is no other." Again in verse 21, "There is no God apart from me, a righteous God and a Savior; there is none but me." The commandment may be expressed this way because our greatest danger is not in substituting a god *for* the Lord , but in trying to synthesize or merge some type of god, or some other type of emphasis, *with* the Lord.

God is saying in this commandment, "If you want to be the happiest, the best adjusted, the most successful person that you can possibly be, you must keep Me alone at the top of your affection."

Here is the basis for all morality. If God is supreme and no competitors are permitted, then there will be no higher standard of obligation and no deeper level of commitment.

The Bible mentions this commandment more than any other of the Ten Commandments. Why is it of paramount importance?

This commandment is first in order to establish the foundational principle that devotion to God is the heart out of which all other laws grow; and if this principle is mastered first, the struggle that might be involved in obeying the other nine is already half won.

Life, too, is not worth living when one does not have a God worth serving. In reality, every person worships a god of some kind. The god worshiped may not be the God of the Bible, but there is always something venerated by every person.

There is but one basic freedom that all of us are given. It is the freedom to determine which god or gods we are going to worship. After that, the god or the thing that we choose to worship will determine what we become.

What is it then that happens to us if we put anything in the place reserved exclusively for God, or accept something in addition to Him?

The thesis of this book is that we hurt ourselves when we worship other gods. In the words of Jeremiah it causes our "own ruin" (7:6 NASB). This same prophet also affirmed that God was saying of the people, "I will give them singleness of heart and action, so that they will always fear me for their own good and the good of their children after them" (Jeremiah 32:39).

So this first commandment targets the four most commonly substituted options to worshiping God alone. They are:

Atheism	(we must have a god),
Internal idolatry	(we must have a heart that has only the Lord as God),
Polytheism	(we must have the Lord alone), and
Formalism	(we must love, reverence, and serve the Lord God with all our heart, soul, strength, and mind).

The people of ancient history had their gods; they recognized them as gods, they called them by name, and made them represent a function important to a happy life. Some of them were: Athena, the goddess of wisdom; Bacchus, the god of wine; Baal, the god of nature and procreation; Serapis, the bull, the god of productivity; Mammon, the god of money; Venus, Aphrodite, and Diana, the goddesses of sex; Aton, the sun, the god of life; and other countless tribal gods.

Today we use different names for these "powers." We don't refer to Athena; we venerate knowledge. We don't name Bacchus; we just worship alcohol. We don't recognize Baal; we just worship sex as a hedonistic expression. We don't talk about Serapis; it's just fertility. Mention isn't made about the god Mammon; we just call it money. Aton is not named, but the sun is worshiped on the beach; Venus, Aphrodite, and Diana are not very common names; we just refer to sex. The name of the god is not important to the Lord. What is worshiped is.

How are we damaged when we allow one of these forces to take too great a place in our life? How are we affected when this commandment is ignored? A disregard for this commandment leads to the following three major losses.

The Loss of Unity

Our oneness is God's plan.

During the sixth century before Christ, when Israel was experiencing exile and hope was about exhausted, Ezekiel was told by the Lord, "I will give them an undivided heart and put a new spirit in them" (11:19).

Though there were many experiences of Israel in the wilderness that tended to be divisive to the nation, the "glue" that provided cohesive force for the tribes of Israel was her worship of the one and only true God. It was this truth that kept the nation from disintegrating. When they began to depart from this basic theological principle, confusion and frustration followed.

When the Bible mentions that the Lord is "a jealous God," the meaning is that He is jealous of our best interest. God is hurt by people diluting their worship of Him not only because by doing so they have disobeyed Him. Rather He knows that when people fail to hold Him alone in highest regard, their lives tend to come apart.

A divided house cannot stand.

Matthew tells us of an occasion when Jesus restored sight and voice to a blind mute who was demon possessed. When the Pharisees heard about it, they affirmed that Jesus was working "by Beelzebub, the prince of demons." Jesus responded that this could not be possible, for Satan could not drive out Satan. Then He said, "Every kingdom divided against itself will be ruined, and every city or household divided against itself will not stand" (Matthew 12:25).

The principle involved here is that if our ultimate allegiance is divided, our unity is fractured, our wholeness is diluted, our view is clouded, and our force is weakened. There can only be one ultimate priority in life.

From excavations at the town of Nuzu, near the modern city of Kirkuk in Iraq, comes a legal document dating from about 1400 B.C. It contains a father's last will and testament to his sons. In it he commanded his sons not to make other gods. To ensure that they would not, he informed them that he would deposit his idols with his oldest son so that all his sons would be united through the worship of the family gods at the home of the chief heir. The text reads, "After I die, my sons shall not make gods, my gods I leave with my eldest son."

The father recognized the importance of unity in the family and tried to prevent more gods from being brought in by any member of it. What this father could not see was that by adding some other god to a number already present was a much smaller step than adding a second god when there had only been one.

In the *Bible Knowledge Commentary* (p. 274) is found this comment on Deuteronomy 6:4.

This verse has been called the *SHEMA* from the Hebrew word translated *hear*. The statement in this verse is the basic theological statement of Judaism. The verse means that the Lord (*Yahweh*) is totally unique. He alone is God. Because of this, the Israelites could have a sense of security that was totally impossible for their polytheistic neighbors. The "gods" of the ancient Near East were rarely thought of as acting in harmony. Each god was unpredictable and morally capricious. So a pagan worshiper could never be sure that his loyalty to one god would serve to protect him from the unbridled wrath of another. The monotheistic doctrine of the Israelites lifted them out of this insecurity since they had to deal with only one God, who dealt with them by a revealed consistent righteous standard.

We cannot serve two masters.

Jesus made it very clear how impossible it is for one to serve two masters, for He said, "Either he will hate the one and love the other, or he will be devoted to the one and despise the other" (Matthew 6:24).

One who tries to serve two masters can never be totally loyal to one. At best he is destined to be no better than halfhearted to either. He cannot develop the force of spirit required to give maximum allegiance to only one. He will inevitably be torn by conflicting loyalties.

Here we should emphasize that the number one differs from all other numbers, not in degree only, but more importantly in kind. There is more essential difference between one and two than there is between two and any other number. It is the number two that first breaks the unity of the one. The step from two to three then is relatively slight. There is, however, an enormous step that separates one from two.

In our language we preserve the importance of the one over the many in the use of singular and plural. The noun form for one is different from the form for two, but there is no difference in the noun form used for two and any other number.

For example, a man who has two wives and a man who has three wives are in the same class as a man who has twenty-five wives. They are all "polygamists." However, the man who has one wife lives in a decidedly different class from all the rest. We say he is a "monogamist." Of necessity, all polygamists have to divide their attention, their affection, and their loyalty. But the man with one wife can be wholly loyal to her alone. This is the way God planned it. He knew that one who worships Him alone will find it more normal to love one wife or husband alone.

Double-mindedness brings instability.

When a person worships some thing or some one in addition to God, he soon develops a double-mindedness. And James tells us, "A double-minded man [is] unstable in all his ways" (1:8).

The principle involved here is that nothing diluted can have the same effect as full strength. Nothing divided can be as directed, as forceful, as strong, as valid, as compelling, or as complete as what is undivided.

The worship of only one God then is essential to one's unity—one's physical, mental, emotional, and spiritual health and well-being. For us to be comfortable with our lives, our world, and ourselves our priorities must line up.

The teeter-totter board operates on the point of a fulcrum. There must be only one, placed near the center of the board for it to work properly. It is impossible to work with more than one fulcrum, for the second one keeps the board from moving at all.

God is the only effective fulcrum in life. He gives proper balance and correct focus. He also provides proper alignment and adds to our effectiveness.

Notice another fact about the fulcrum. It can help redistribute weight. If the fulcrum is placed properly, and if the pry bar is long enough, almost any weight can be lifted. Theoretically, if a person had a fulcrum properly placed, and a plank long enough, it would be possible to lift the world.

The Loss of Identity

When there is a dividing of one's allegiance, the direction taken is one that leads to schizophrenia or "split personality." When loyalty is divided and oneness is broken, one is then led directly to a blurred identity.

Hypocrisy is often the end result of a divided loyalty. God did not make anyone to be a hypocrite. But when a divided allegiance is permitted on the highest level, it filters down. It becomes easier to "put on," to pretend, or to allow the counterfeit. And if the artificial is taken to be real by other people, then the person thinks, "Why should I bother with being real? I can hide that. I can be a good actor. I can take on many roles. This means I can manipulate people."

It doesn't take long before the mind of a hypocrite asks himself, "Who are you anyway? Are you who you think you are or is the pretense the real you?" Then follows an inner battle with the now divided self, struggling to decide who has the real identity.

This may well be why movie stars have such difficulty with having happy marriages and why divorce is so common. They spend so much of their lives "being" other people that they soon don't really know who they are themselves. They have multiple identities.

In the *American Standard Version*, Jeremiah asks, "Do they provoke me to anger? saith Jehovah; do they not provoke themselves, to the confusion of their own faces?" (7:19).

Paul tells Timothy how he is constantly remembering him in his prayers day and night, and how he longs to see him. He recalls the young man's tears, and the old apostle is "reminded of your sincere faith . . ." (2 Timothy 1:5). The Greek term Paul uses is, transliterated, *anhypocritos*. This word comes into English as *nonhypocritical*.

True sincerity is transparent. The one who has it is not plagued by another personality hiding in some corner waiting for its chance to come on stage. Hypocrisy simply cannot find a comfortable place to dwell in a sincere person. It demands a dwelling where there is plenty of insincerity, pretense, and duplicity.

Confusion reigns.

One of the more prominent Proverbs is "Acquitting the guilty and condemning the innocent—the Lord detests them both" (17:15).

When some other loyalty is allowed to compete with loyalty to the Lord, other areas of life are affected. Conflicting loyalties permitted at the core of life cause tentacles of similar infection to spread into other areas.

One end result is often an inability to think deeply about matters of importance, causing one to find it difficult to make an important and valued decision. There is lacking a capacity to see a clear way ahead in a crisis, for there is an inability to focus full attention in one direction.

A divided, bifurcated life leads to confusion and perplexity. It can ultimately lead to such a chaos of moral judgment as to make anarchy almost certain.

A divided life feeds on itself. Once a division is permitted in the space where God alone will fit, a person then tries to fill it with other things. All attempts to put anything there along with God is like the proverbial "square peg in a round hole." It won't fit!

When we permit anything to compete with God at the helm of life, we then try to unite the other interests with God. This causes God to lose top priority. Self has to take over. Then in order to support that rule, self begins to elevate things or people to positions of more importance. God is given less and less attention. When things or people assume the place of God, they soon become a god.

Most of our lives are made up of the unscheduled stimuli, which often makes us respond with an unplanned reaction. We often do not have enough time to condition our responses. The "real" person, who on one occasion is supposed to hide, appears. The "other" person, who needs to appear in order to maintain contrived identity, doesn't show and confusion takes over a larger role in life.

Proper order is reversed.

Isaiah focused on the end result of such confusion being allowed to grow. Assessment of what is right and what is wrong in any given situation gets turned around. He says, "Woe to those who call evil good and good evil, who put darkness for light and light for darkness, who put bitter for sweet, and sweet for bitter. Woe to those who are wise in their own eyes and clever in their own sight!" (Isaiah 5:20-21).

When one attempts to fill the void in life with something in addition to God, evil and good get disordered. What is good and what is evil, what is right and what is wrong gets confused and then good and evil, right and wrong reverse themselves. For when we sense we are losing control of our life, we try to use whatever we can to maintain control. If we think error will adequately serve that purpose, then maintaining control in all situations becomes more important than preserving truth at all costs. If error gives us temporary relief from losing control, what seemed to be wrong before now appears to be right and the confusion process is exacerbated.

Mixed utterances.

One of the first places where not allowing God sole possession of top spot in life shows up is in one's conversation. James notes, "From the same mouth come both blessing and cursing. . . . Does a fountain send out from the same opening both fresh and bitter water?" (3:10-11 NASB).

When God is pushed aside from His throne, He then becomes an easy target. Instead of being reserved for prayer and worship, His name is soon used for all kinds of pledges, oaths, and even swearing, further confusing us as to whom or what God is. Is He the supreme Being of the Universe, or is He what at any given moment props up an individual on his throne and makes him feel he is his own lord?

Convictions are lost.

Ignoring this commandment leads to another most damaging danger. What were rock solid convictions now are lost in an easy tolerance.

When one engages in pretense, for that moment he is something other than he really is. Then he finds it necessary for that length of time to become more tolerant with himself so the added "personality," the alternate, the other, the additional can seem genuine. He momentarily must allow his tolerance to include this deviation.

The constant tendency of the people in Old Testament times was to mingle with the local Canaanite population. Not being guided by divine truth, the Canaanites based their practices on observation and experience. Being mostly farmers, they had to know and understand the weather patterns. Rains did not come in the summer—only in the fall through the spring. Rain was absolutely essential. Fertility became all-important to them.

They concocted a system of beliefs that rain was in reality Baal's semen coming down to fertilize the earth. They could make Baal happy if they would get involved in similar activity. Prostitution, bestiality, and all kinds of sexual aberrations became common place. They were deemed "necessary" if life was to blossom and continue.

So now we have a Hebrew farmer settling down next to a Canaanite farmer who has visited his "sacred" prostitutes, he has played around with other men, he has had sex with his animals, he may well have gone out to drop some of his own semen on his ground to make it more fertile. He has expressed himself sexually every way he could. Every time he has felt that electric surge going through his body, he considered it proof that Baal was blessing him.

The fall rains are late in coming one year. He is aware his Hebrew neighbor doesn't believe in what he considers his most effective system to bring the needed water. I can hear his condemnation shouted across the hillside: "It's your fault we have this drought! Baal is angry with you and I'm suffering as a result."

The natural temptation of this Hebrew farmer would not be to give up the worship of his God; it is rather the temptation to add to his faith in a tolerant manner, thus producing an infected and diluted worship which would eat at every strand of its fabric like mildew.

But to him he is only being liberal. He was inclined to ask, "Why can't I be tolerant and include some of the better aspects of Baal worship with my worship? After all, fertility is a necessity of life. Without it everything ceases to be. Why should I not say 'this and' instead of 'either or?'"

Elijah saw the folly of just that kind of a divided allegiance. On the occasion of the contest on Mt. Carmel between him and the Baal priests, he told the people of Israel who hadn't totally given up the worship of God, but who had blended it with the worship of Baal, "How long will you waver between [literally "limp on"] the two divided opinions? If the LORD is God, follow Him; but if Baal is God, follow him" (1 Kings 18:21).

In his book, *Living Under God's Law*, Robert Ingram says, "The sober truth is that we cannot make a decent civilization by following the modern fashion of tolerance with a patronizing spirit. We must have a burning faith which will change men's lives."

Elton Trueblood said, "Power comes not by supposing that one view is as good as another, but by finding, in honest inquiry, what the objective truth seems to be, and then following it with stubborn courage tempered by humility. There can be no cutting edge that is not narrow."

The great question, now as always, is not whether we shall be "religious," but which religion we shall prize and foster. There have always been many false religions, but only one true one.

Great advances come in culture, not when all distinctions are blurred in a hazy and jovial good will, but when sharp distinctions are made, distinctions dictated by the truth.

"Tolerance" is the key word for success today. People boast about their own type something like this: "Every one has a right to his own view," or, "We have to separate politics from religion and let religion be a private matter."

"Sure! That's valid!" is a quick response. But will such a view stand up under analysis? Does one have a right to his own view if it includes violence? Did the Nazis of World War II have a right to their own view? Is a religious fanatical Muslim free to his own view if it goads him into a bombing that takes the lives of innocent people?

The freedom of religion idea for many is little more than "glorified indifference." Some people espouse "freedom *of* religion" because they want to be "free *from* religion." To them religion is unimportant. What they call "freedom of religion" goes something like this for the non-Christian: "For the life of me, I cannot understand why anybody wants to do anything so futile as to worship something you can't see, feel, or touch, like God. He probably doesn't exist anyway. It sure is a silly way to spend a Sunday morning in a stuffy old church when you can unwind from a hectic week at your job by sleeping in or by watching something interesting on T.V. But I'm very tolerant about these things. I wouldn't do a thing to stop him."

For the churchgoer, it issues in a nonchalant attitude. An issue of importance comes up; the reaction is: "Oh, I'm a very open-minded person. I don't care one way or the other about that! I can accept it either way!"

A diluted life leads to a confusion of moral values, an indifference to issues of importance, a lessening of personal convictions and an ultimate weakening of identity.

The Loss of Position

Humans are supreme in the world.

One of God's instructions to Adam and Eve was, "Rule over the fish of the sea and the birds of the air and over every living creature that moves on the ground" (Genesis 1:28). The Psalmist in 8:5 tells us we are created a little lower than the "heavenly beings." While the Hebrew word *Elohim* is occasionally translated "angels," thus "heavenly beings," more often it means "God."

Positionally, we were created with only God above us.

Worshipers must always worship something above them. For me to worship is to admit my inferiority to the object I worship—and the superiority of that object over me. We do not worship "down." We must worship "up." Above us is only God. Beneath us is everything else.

For us then, worship is due no other one but God—not an angel, not a government, not a heavenly body, not the rain, not the fire, not another person, certainly not an animal, or money, or sex, or fame, or popularity. Only God alone.

The Second Commandment

You shall not make for yourself an idol in the form of anything in heaven above or on the earth beneath or in the waters below (Exodus 20:4).

Sustaining a Right Relationship with God

There was only a period of 19 years left before Judah's captivity would become a reality at the hands of Nebuchadnezzar. Jeremiah told the people that seventy years of Babylonian exile was certain (25:11). In hopes of a few turning to the LORD on a personal level, Jeremiah gave the divine message, "You did not listen to me . . . and you have provoked me with what your hands have made, and you have brought harm to yourselves" (v. 7).

There is nothing easier to understand than the process by which an idol comes to be regarded as divine. God is a spirit and a power generally invisible to the eyes of humankind. We are sense-directed people; it is very hard for some to think about—and to worship—an unseen God, who is to be seen only with an eye of faith.

So there is always a desire to make it a little easier for people to worship by giving them something they can look at while worshiping. An image of some kind is made, meant to remind people of God when they look at it, so that they can better focus their thoughts on the God for whom it stands.

But bit by bit the image ceases to *represent* God and begins to *take the place* of God. To the mind of that worshiper, God has not left the process; but when the *cult of the thing* replaces the *meaning of the thing,* idolatry has occurred.

One who venerates a thing for which an object stands, and one who venerates the object itself are in two different classes. One is a worshiper; the other is an idolater.

The process is not abrupt. It goes gradually like this:
*   There is first *remembrance* of
*   Then comes *respect* for
*   Then follows a *veneration* of
*   And ultimately there is a *worship* of

This process often happened in Old Testament times. In their wilderness days, the Israelites were attacked by fiery serpents. On the instructions of God,

Moses made a bronze serpent and set it up on a pole. Those who had been bitten and who looked at the bronze serpent were healed (Numbers 21:6-9).

Centuries afterwards, the bronze serpent object makes another brief appearance. This time Hezekiah finds it necessary to beat it into pieces because the people had been burning incense to it (2 Kings 18:4). Originally, the object had been meant to be a *reminder* of God; but little by little, it *became* a god.

It would seem that if the first commandment was effective (**Have no other gods besides me, or in addition to me**), there would be no need for a commandment against worshiping another god in the form of an image.

It is God's desire to give us convictions to do what is right and not to do what is wrong, even when no one else will know. Thus, the reason for the first commandment is to preserve internal worship.

The second commandment looks at another problem. Internal worship needs external direction. Thus we find value in those objects which help us focus on God. However, by having something external to view, we also run the risk of treating that item as an idol. The greater risk is this: the devil uses external stimuli to bring about internal control.

The problem.

God created all things beneath himself. He created angels whom He uses to guide the nations. But one of them, Lucifer, in pride fell from his created estate. He wanted to make himself independent of his Maker and compete with his own Creator.

Revelation 12:9 tells us Satan "leads the whole world astray." His method is to make all people rebels, to get them to revolt against God's control over their lives. If he can get one to develop a mutinous spirit over any aspect of life, he has that person well on the way to becoming a rebel. Once that process of rebellion starts, the rebel is never satisfied until he can arrogate to himself *all* power and bow to no other.

So the devil, unable to usurp God in heaven, has now been involved in a millennia-long battle to even the score with God on the battleground of the world. He wants to "get even" with God.

His insidious method is encapsulated in one word: "totalitarian." He wants total control and all movements toward total control, whether of the individual, which is the immediate battleground for all of us, or by economic domination of society, or totalitarian control of government.

The devil will not be satisfied until he has total control of the world through despotic leadership so that he can bring on the anti-Christ. From his viewpoint, to have his own "Christ" will be the ultimate "slap in the face" of God. That "Christ" will be his "son" who will try to set up his kingdom on this earth.

It is characteristic of Satan-controlled hearts to have only the kind of a god they can control. If they make their god, they can more easily manipulate him. They can then make sure he does not condemn them, or accuse them, or make them feel guilty.

In general it is more human to opt for the visible over the invisible. Any attempt to bring God into the visible world will inevitably reduce Him to a smaller, manageable limit.

In the wilderness, Aaron's attempt seemed honorable (Exodus 32:6, 22-24). He was synthesizing the worship of the calf, to which he had been exposed in Egypt, with the worship of the LORD. His effort seems not to have been intended to replace God with the golden calf god. Gods of the Near East often are found placed on top of a bull calf as if the calf was a pedestal.

Over half a millennium later, Jeroboam also was threatened with a fear that while his people would be politically tied to him, they would be religiously tied to Jerusalem, now the capital of a different country. His solution was to erect two golden calves; one was set up at the southern most city of Bethel, and the other at the northern most city of Dan (1 Kings 12:26-33).

It would seem both Aaron and Jeroboam were trying to be accommodating to the people in their situations by focusing attention on the space above the calf, rather than the calf itself. (Notice the translation of the word *Elohim* in Exodus 32:4. It can be translated, God, singular with a capital G: "This your God, O Israel" rather than "gods," plural with a small g.) Of course it is clear that Jeroboam had gone a little farther, burning incense to two calves. But he still held the biblical feasts, simply moving them back thirty days, so that for example, his country would be celebrating the Tabernacle festival a month later than when Jerusalem was celebrating theirs (1 Kings 12:33).

It should be noted here that Jeroboam would probably not have been as successful with his greater deviation if Aaron had not set the precedence with his less innocuous deviation back at Mt. Sinai.

These men, certainly Aaron if not Jeroboam, may well have reasoned that God's concentrated presence was in the Holy of Holies atop a box called the "ark of the covenant," on what was called "the mercy seat." So why not localize His presence above a calf, thinking of the LORD as standing on top of that calf? In reality they were trying to restrict God to a limited and confined place.

They even may have reasoned, "Our God is more important than the calf which is under His feet." Other peoples did this with their deities. Archaeological discoveries have revealed rock-cut reliefs of the gods of people from Old Testament times. They generally look like men. Several have been presented as standing on the top of a small bull calf.

God wanted to be thought near His people, so He dwelt in the most Holy Place in the Tabernacle. To keep that piece of furniture from being worshiped, He commanded that it be kept behind a curtain, away from everyone but the High Priest, who could enter the room only once a year on the Day of Atonement.

God required this arrangement to keep people from commonizing Him and to help preserve the mystery of His presence. It seems probable that otherwise the people would have too easily given the veneration due Him to the Ark itself. And that would have been one long step into idolatry.

What might be called "idolatry in the mind" always precedes an idol of wood, or stone, or metal. While in our day, and especially in this country, the second step is not often taken, there is ever as much idolatry of the mind. To be sure, this second commandment is just as much needed today as it was three-and-one-half millennia ago.

Any form of idolatry, internal or external, is injurious to one's spiritual health for the following five reasons.

God cannot be confined to a small visible area.

Isaiah succinctly expresses the utter folly of externally expressing the idolatry of the mind (44:14-20). He scornfully pictures a man taking a piece of wood, using some of it to make a fire to warm himself, some of it to cook his food, and with the remainder of it carving out a god.

Our God is simply too big to be confined in a small item or to a small space. It limits Him and makes Him meaningless and helpless.

In the apocryphal book, "The Letter of Jeremiah," is found this description of idol making: "The gods who are idols have got to be dusted like furniture every morning. Their faces are blackened by the temple smoke, and the bats and the swallows and the birds and even the cats settle on them.

"Set them upright, and they cannot move; tip them over, and they cannot raise themselves. They are no more than that which a carpenter or a goldsmith made them to be.

"If there is fire in a temple, the priests can flee, but the gods can only stay and be burned. The temple has to be locked up at nights, lest robbers steal the gods and their ornaments. Strong men strip them and go off with the booty, and they can do nothing to help themselves. They are no better than a scarecrow or a thorn-bush in a garden on which every bird sits. They are no better than a dead body, cast out in the darkness."

Idolatry upsets the balance of life.

God endowed us with the five senses: seeing, hearing, feeling, smelling, and tasting. The loss of any one of these limits a person in many ways. In the way God designed that He be worshiped, all five senses are to be used. Too often idolatry causes one to lose the delicate balance, depending too much on sight, or touch, or another of the senses.

Idolatry reduces God to a limited space.

In Old Testament times people were tempted to think of their god as a god of a certain people or a given territory. A deity was often thought to dwell among a certain people. For one god to have a universal character seems not to have occurred to them as a possibility. The Egyptians seem to have come the nearest when Pharaoh Akhenaton tried to get all of Egypt to worship the solar disc alone. The country rebelled against the idea and the priests caused a return to many gods.

The information we are given in Jonah shows that the sailors on the boat, likely from different countries and employed by a Phoenician company, had brought their national gods with them.

When the storm came, all the sailors were praying to their gods except Jonah, who was sleeping in the hold of the ship. Having been discovered by the ship's captain, he was awakened and told, "Get up and call on your god! Maybe he will take notice of us, and we will not perish" (Jonah 1:6).

The superstitious captain was fearful of perhaps all national gods, and he didn't want to offend any one of them. All the sailors became "extremely frightened" when they learned of Jonah's disobedience to his God. They tried to avoid having to take Jonah's advice of throwing him overboard, but finally they had to comply with his admonition.

While Jonah learned that his disobedience could cause disastrous results, he still begrudged that the LORD would even offer salvation to any other people but the Jews. He likely thought that the Assyrians had their own god. Why should they be offered salvation by the LORD, especially after their rampant cruelty?

Perhaps one might reason, "I appreciate the information about Jonah, his disobedience, his biases, his possible belief that his God was a God of the Holy Land, who might ignore his flight from it, but I don't think this 'God of locality' idea has any application to our day." Let's probe that idea a bit.

Consider a situation where a minister, perhaps a rather well-liked pastor, feels he should move to take another church. There are some people who decide that if he leaves, they too will have to leave. The question needs to be asked, "Is their worship centered in God or in humankind?" Are they not making a pastor in effect a totem by saying, "If he isn't the pastor of this church, I cannot worship God here anymore"?

Can God ever be represented only by one person? Is this not limiting Him in ways He never intended to be limited? Has one not taken a giant step toward idolatry in such a situation?

Consider also another way some Christians try to squeeze God into a certain confined space. Because of changing living patterns of a congregation; or because a building is too small to any longer meet the needs of the congregation; or because there is a need to relocate to reach another segment of people; the local church decides it is necessary to sell the present sanctuary and build a new one in another location.

Some oppose such a move mainly because of a long-standing tradition, fueled by the length of time the old building has been in service, and the countless memories of what occurred there. There may even be some opposition based on past spiritual experiences that occurred at the altar, or special revivals held in bygone days.

I recall vividly a time when the church of my childhood decided to relocate to a better site in the city. I must admit that I had a sinking nostalgic feeling about the whole situation. I had to tell myself, God is not a God of only one specific place. He not only could, but also would, be in the new building at the new place. If I thought otherwise, I was restricting God. For I was saying, "God, you don't want to leave this building to go to another. You can't be there, God. You can only bless in this building. You can only be worshiped here."

Any attempt to confine God's presence inside a specific building, or to restrict His effectiveness by believing He only wants to operate out of a restricted area, is another monumental step taken toward idolatry. And that is a violation of the second commandment.

Idolatry can begin with association.

For the past forty years I have been taking people to the land of Israel in an effort to help them enhance their faith by, as we often say, "walking in the footsteps of Jesus," and seeing the land He helped to be termed "Holy Land."

Nazareth was a backward city before the Lord made it notable. There are thousands of lakes in the world more beautiful than the Sea of Galilee, but it was Jesus who gave it greater significance.

Many places can be viewed which were made special because of the traditions of Jesus having been there. Examples are Dominus Flavit, where it is said Jesus wept over Jerusalem; the Stone of Agony, where He prayed the night He was arrested; Golgotha, or Skull Hill, where the tree that held His body was located; the Stone of Unction at the base of Golgotha, on which tradition affirms that His body was prepared for burial after being lowered from the cross.

It is a common sight to see scores of men and women coming to the stone, kneeling before it, rubbing handkerchiefs on it, caressing it with their hands, bowing their heads down to touch it and even kissing it repeatedly.

While only God can look on the heart, it appears these people have given the stone itself a divine character. The stone is venerated because of its association with Jesus, real or imagined.

It is unsettling for many pilgrims to learn that there are two Calvarys and two tombs in Israel connected with Jesus. "Which one do you think is the right one?" I am often asked. My response? Perhaps God wanted us not to know the place for sure. If the place were known with greater certainty, would there not be more worship of the place, rather than worship at the place? Though such can be a veneration of Him at the place, rather than a veneration of the place, the fuzzy line of idolatry is so easily crossed that one can do it without a full awareness of it happening.

Idolatry lifts self to deity status.

Setting limits to God's presence, or to His effectiveness, causes the one who does it to elevate himself almost to the level of a god. The sense of bigness and the importance one feels make him begin to act and speak as though he is God's executive secretary.

If my God only acts and speaks in ways I affirm, then He soon will only follow my every whim and wish. I can manipulate Him. I can control Him. I can make Him look like I want Him to look. I can make Him say what I want Him to say. And before long my importance in my own eyes is so altered from reality that I begin to abridge laws to suit my whims. I then see some acts prohibited in the Bible as not applying to me, for with my God I have special status. He gives me certain permission to do what others are denied. I have now become a god to my God.

I now live in direct violation of Deuteronomy 10:12-13 which says, "And now, O Israel, what does the LORD your God ask of you but to fear the LORD your God, to walk in all his ways, to love him, to serve the LORD your God with all your heart and with all your soul, and to observe the LORD's commands and decrees that I am giving you today for your own good?"

To give an illustration of how this works, let me tell of a certain church, which for years struggled to reach a high number of fifty in attendance. After some time, a young man came to be pastor and almost immediately the attendance climbed into the hundreds. The meteoric rise was so phenomenal that the local district sponsored the young man to speak at church growth conferences, to chronicle his method of attendance building.

After a few years the attendance began to top off and stabilize. Apparently not wanting this to be known outside his congregation, the pastor began to artificially raise the numbers on the monthly reports. Approached later by the vice chairman of the church board about the elevated statistics, the pastor reprimanded him and tried to have him removed from his position and from the membership role.

Opposition to the pastor gained momentum. In time he angrily left, taking part of the church with him to start a new independent church. He asked his followers not to have any dealings with the members who refused to leave the main church, even suggesting they cross the street if necessary to avoid them.

Eventually the pastor was caught in a charge of immorality. He was asked to surrender his credentials. It was later learned he had gone to a bank and had set up a private account which was only available to him personally, and in which he was depositing some money people had intended for the church. Today the pastor is not in the ministry, rather he's occupied selling cars. One of the most perceptive members who lived through the ordeal analyzed the situation as follows: "During the first four years when the church was experiencing the phenomenal growth, the pastor proclaimed 'Look what God is doing!' After that time the report changed to 'Look what God and I are doing!' In the final years it became, 'Look what I am doing!'"

The elevation of self to deity status was obvious to the more discerning. It was very soon after the pastor began to take credit due the Lord that the church began to taper off in growth. And it appears that, to his own mind, the pastor thought he could write his own laws for his conduct concerning financial and moral demeanor. He became his own god and to some degree worshiped himself.

Idolatry lowers God to servant status.

When I lower God and elevate myself, I now must have my God do for me all I want Him to do. Instead of my being here to serve Him, He is there to serve me. My needs and desires are primary. His plans and goals are all bent my way.

Now that self has succeeded in sitting on my own throne, I will remake my God to conform to my desires. I will cut away what I don't like, make archaic what I don't want to recognize, add to where I perceive there is a void, so that eventually I have created my god in my own image and he has become my idol.

In this process I am faced with a dilemma. If my god makes me uncomfortable in any way, it is not I that must change. My god will have to change. I am the measurement to match. My god must rise no higher than I stand. If I am ruthless, my god must allow my ruthlessness, which makes him ruthless too. If I am violent, my god will allow it as normal and expected. If I choose to be irresponsible, my god conveniently looks the other way.

The Solution

The only solution for such situations that point so directly to idolatry is to give God His rightful place in our lives. We must heed the words of Moses, "If . . . you seek the LORD your God, you will find him if you look for him with all your heart and all your soul. . . . For the LORD your God is a merciful God; He will not abandon or destroy you" (Deuteronomy 4:29, 31).

The Third Commandment

You shall not take the name of the LORD your God in vain (Exodus 20:7 NASB).

The psalmist David in speaking of the wicked men affirms, "they speak against You wickedly; Your enemies take Your name in vain" (139:20 NKJV).

For life to have meaning, for opportunities to be possible, for achievements to present themselves, for contentment to occur, for fulfillment to be realized, more depends on the quality of the person than on any given amount of luck. Or to put the truth another way, what happens without us is not nearly as critical to fulfillment as to what happens within us. A viable and close relationship with God is vital, if not essential, for one to obtain and develop quality. The writer of Proverbs put it this way, "The fear of the LORD is a fountain of life" (14:27 NKJV). Similarly, the psalmist expresses, "For with you is the fountain of life; in Your light we see light" (36:9 NKJV).

Relationship must begin with the right introduction, and in Christian theology that is done by conversion. As a proper introduction needs a go-between, one who knows best both parties who want a relationship, so it is with God. Jesus Christ stepped into that chasm dividing us from God, so that the strangeness and unfamiliarity that separated us from the Lord could be bridged.

Once the relationship is established, it is important that neither party do anything to mar or violate that relationship. Each must hold the other in highest regard so that when one refers to the other, that esteem is always evident.

When a man and a woman stand before an altar, they are establishing a marriage relationship based on a pledge made before God that they will honor, respect, and love each other "until death." As long as that pledge is supported by actions on the part of both, the relationship holds. However, if either speaks ill of the other, misrepresents the truth, or violates the pledges, even though the other party may not know of the violation, the relationship is marred to the degree of that violation.

Suppose either mate makes the other one think there is no other person occupying the same level of relationship, yet the truth is otherwise. The relationship cannot be based on how much the faithful spouse knows or does not know. It is based on what are the actual facts, not what are assumed to be the facts. Notice the following diagram.

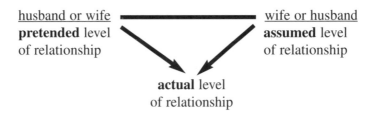

A relationship with God is similar, the main difference being that God is never ignorant about the facts. He always knows everything. But the relationship is more at the level of the actions taken than the words spoken.

James states, "With the tongue we praise our Lord and Father, and with it we curse men, who have been made in God's likeness. Out of the same mouth come praise and cursing. My brothers, this should not be. Can both fresh water and salt water flow from the same spring? My brothers, can a fig tree bear olives, or a grapevine bear figs? Neither can a salt spring produce fresh water" (3:9-12).

The water that flows from a fountain is only as pure as its worst contaminant. It is not possible to be badly tainted for one person and entirely pure for another.

With respect to our relationship with God, it is not possible to speak His name in worship on Sunday, then use the same name in profanity on Monday and expect to continue at the same level of relationship. The use of the profanity infects one's whole relationship with God, including worship on Sunday. Of course, one may *act* in worship as though there is a relationship with God, but doing so makes the *actor* a hypocrite.

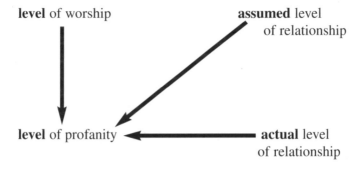

Since a hypocrite has violated a trust to always consider God's name too holy to be used in any other context than is deserving of Him, the only prayer he can pray, using God's name, that actually reaches God is a prayer of repentance. It is not possible to be on God's side one day and on Satan's side the next any more than it is possible for a member of a team to play on one side for one quarter in a game and on the other side for the next quarter.

The Jews refrained from even vocalizing God's name, feeling such would commonize Him. Once while reading Hebrew orally in one of my graduate university classes, I came to the name for God, *Elohim*, in the text and dutifully read it aloud. Immediately, the professor came off the platform on which he stood. Clapping his hands in disapproval, he stopped in front of me. I asked what I had done. He told me I had verbalized the ineffable Name. I protested, "But you told me to read the text!" He made me understand that I was to substitute the words "Ha Shem" for God, meaning "the Name." So I read, "In the beginning the Name created the heavens and the earth."

Many Jews refrain from even writing the name for God, preferring rather to indicate it by G-d. For the Christian this seems to be going a bit far on the other side of the spectrum, for while God is interested in how one *says* His name, He is more concerned about how one *regards* His name.

The Hebrews attached great significance to the meaning of names. Any name beginning with a Je or Jo, such as Jeremiah, Jehoshaphat, or Joseph, or ending in an -iah, such as Isaiah or Nehemiah, has God's name in its formation. The same was true of place names, especially if a significant manifestation had been made there. Special reverence is always to be paid to the name of God as divine, for it represents His person and His character. So when one's character changed because of an encounter with God, his name had to reflect that change.

While this commandment is usually cited as a rule against profanity or vulgarity, this does not exhaust its meaning; it has a much broader application.

The key words here are "in vain" which in the Hebrew literally mean "in unreality."

Human statements do often contain inaccuracy and falsehood, intentionally or unintentionally. Knowing this, occasionally a person may feel a statement needs verification. The Lord does not object to His name being used for such a purpose. In Exodus 22:10-11 He permitted the use of His name to affirm the truth of human witness, and thereby become the inspiration of a concerted effort to always be truthful. When people gave their word under such an oath, they were to be taken so seriously that even when no corroborative evidence supported what was said, trust was to be placed in it.

The admonition in Deuteronomy 6:13 "Fear the LORD your God, serve him only and take your oaths in his name," indicates that God intended His name to be used specifically to improve our integrity and honesty by committing ourselves to it and to all that it stands for.

When one mentioned another person's name it was as though that person's presence was being invoked. This promoted a greater concern for not saying anything about a person that one would not say if that person were physically present.

Let us explore the two main ways we can disregard God's name and how we hurt ourselves by taking His name in vain.

In a Promise or a Pledge

This commandment prohibits taking the name of God in vain in a promise or a pledge, with no intention of keeping it, or making a promise in the name of God and afterwards breaking it because it was uncomfortable or inconvenient to keep it.

If God is holy, then His name must also be holy. If His name is holy it must never be used in a frivolous manner to testify to anything that is untrue, insincere, inaccurate, empty, or idle.

God abhors dishonesty in any form, and if His name is used to make a person look better than he or she really is, to blanket or cover over an evil heart, He is doing the person a disservice to approve of such a practice. God never looks alone at a confession; He wants to know if that confession is but a cloak under which an evil heart is hiding.

This commandment represents other such prohibitions in the Bible. In Leviticus 19:12 we are commanded by God not to "swear falsely by my name." In Jeremiah 5:2 the prophet condemns those who say, "As surely as the LORD lives," yet swear falsely.

Elton Trueblood notes, "The worst blasphemy is not profanity, but lip service."

In Unnecessary Conversation

Involved in this commandment also is the uttering of God's name unnecessarily in common conversation. There is a world of difference in saying, "by the help of God, I'll do that," and "by God I'll do that." While both can mean the same, the second is the popularly used expression for swearing, and is now not used to invoke God's help at all.

How We Hurt Ourselves by Using the LORD's Name in Vain

Then the question follows, how can we hurt ourselves when we are talking about a matter of simply saying words?

We trivialize life.

We will hurt ourselves by *trivializing life*. We do that when we do not consider words we say as important enough to express the truth, so we think we have to emphasize them by oath taking.

God is so committed to our genuineness that He cannot countenance any artificiality in deed or in word. One might think this commandment is unneeded since the ninth one prohibits lying. But what is being prohibited here is different.

It may well be we need this commandment even more than in biblical times because of our reliance on the *written* word, and less on the *spoken* word.

During most of the time in Old Testament history, only professional scribes were trained to write. When writing was needed, their services were engaged much the way we might use a notary today. Because of this, much more significance and importance was put on the spoken word. It was not used flippantly; what was said was considered binding not only on the speaker, but also on all who were affected by that word.

Let us look at the case of Jephthah in Judges 11. This judge was conscious that a tremendous responsibility had been thrust upon him to try to free the Israelites from the Ammonite oppression that had been going on for several years. The tribes on the east side of Jordan, in Gilead, had put their trust in him.

Notice that Jephthah tried to use diplomacy to solve the problem, but that had failed (Judges 11:12-22). He now knew he would have to fight, so he pulled out all stops. He verbally vowed to God that if the LORD would help him win the battle over the children of Ammon (v. 30), then "whatever comes out of the door of my house to meet me when I return in triumph . . . will be the LORD's, and I will sacrifice it as a burnt offering" (v. 31).

Many are quick to affirm that Jephthah actually sacrificed his daughter on the altar as one would an animal, citing that in that society, tainted with paganism, he did not know any better.

But nothing is more abhorred in the Bible than child sacrifice. Again and again the Lord condemned it and warned against it.

Some years ago I went to Carthage in Tunisia in North Africa to do archaeological work in what the Bible calls *Tophets*. These were child burial grounds used for children who had been sacrificed to the pagan god Baal, known to us from the Bible as one of the many that demanded child sacrifice. It was an experience that was most unsettling. I have come across many burials in my work through the years. None were so moving as when I experienced excavating the cremated remains of children whose lives were robbed from them by a heathen system of belief. If worshipers did not please Baal, this god of nature, storms, earthquakes, rain, and fertility, he would become angry with them and cause a famine or some other devastation. So, in order to appease him, they took their most loved and most cherished offspring. After slitting his throat, they cremated him as an offering to Baal. We found hundreds and hundreds of them, along with a tombstone that told of the dedication of this child to Baal, at times even carving out a most grotesque picture of the god on the stone.

Nowhere do we find God "winking" at such a practice because of the ignorance of the people, something He sometimes did with other cultural practices like the marriage of multiple wives to alleviate barrenness or to stress influence and affluence.

But in the case of Jephthah, the Hebrew text does not demand it, for the word that is normally translated "and" in verse 31 occasionally should be translated "or." Jephthah knew there was a possibility that his daughter might come out. His hope, however, was that the animal he was keeping in the house until it bore its young, would come out. Thus, he promises the Lord that if his daughter comes out, she will be the Lord's "or" (if it is an animal) "I will sacrifice it as a burnt offering."

The more important point is that he makes a verbal pledge that he feels he cannot break under any circumstance. He lived in a day when the spoken word was binding. The bottom line: Jephthah did as he vowed (v. 39).

Another incident of the importance of the spoken word can be found in Genesis 27. Rebekah wanted Jacob to get his father's deathbed blessing, while Isaac was intent on giving it to Esau, who though he was a twin, was the older of the two boys.

Jacob then pretended to be Esau, even allowing his mother to put the skin of a young goat on his arms and his neck (v. 16). And though the nearly blind Isaac suspected something was amiss, he still gave Jacob the oral blessing, not knowing of the duplicity. Jacob had hardly left the room (v. 30), when Esau returned from his hunt and sought Isaac's blessing. Isaac "trembled violently" (v. 33) when he began to realize how he had been duped by Jacob. Esau plaintively asked, "Haven't you reserved any blessing for me?" (v. 36).

But Isaac answered in verse 37, "I have made him lord over you, . . . So what can I possibly do for you, my son?" Esau pleaded, "Do you have only one blessing, my father? Bless me, too, my father!" (v. 38). But that was not possible, for the words, even though uttered under what was assumed different circumstances, could not be altered.

While we would not want to return to that day when more emphasis had to be given to the spoken word, especially since there was so little knowledge of writing available, still it might be better if we paid more attention to making our words more creditable.

Have you heard someone say, "Come and see me sometime"? But it is known that that person really doesn't want you to visit. Or have you had someone ask you, "How are you"? But they really don't care how you are. "I'm praying for you" is another phrase some may glibly say, but the words are not based in fact. Words are often empty and do not say at all what the person really means. God wanted to prevent this from happening because words are of vital importance to the general impression one makes in life.

Today even in court proceedings, it is but natural for a judge or an attorney to ask, "Is it in writing?" What is said does not have nearly the creditability as does the written word. As one's words are thus weakened, the Lord is not pleased, for when our word is not believable, we feel the need of stressing it with an oath.

It seems when we begin to get careless about our relationship to God, we begin to feel a vacuum in the validity of our word. When we make a statement, we increasingly feel the need to add to it with something like, "I'm really telling the truth!" What we are saying is, "Sometimes when I speak I don't tell the truth."

The less genuine a person feels about himself, the more he feels a need to pull in the name of God or of Jesus to underscore what is said.

Such a practice develops a shallowness in our lives. It cheapens our word and encourages us to make statements, pledges, or invitations we do not consider important, serious, or significant. That reaction produces a superficiality that at times makes serious and important things trivial.

The Essenes of the Dead Sea Scroll community held that "he who cannot be believed without swearing is condemned already."

William Ward believes, "Profanity is the use of strong words by weak people."

What can be said for people who are not genuine Christians, but who go to church and sing songs like, "All the way my Savior leads me," or "Take my life and let it be, consecrated Lord to Thee"? There has to be a disconnection between their minds and their tongues.

James 5:12 tells us, "Above all, my brothers, do not swear—not by heaven or by earth or by anything else. Let your 'Yes' be yes, and your 'No,' no, or you will be condemned." The idea for us here is that we should express truth on all occasions so we will not need the name of God to verify our statements.

We lose God's closeness.

Quite concerned about the increasing use of profanity among his troops, George Washington wrote to them these words: "We can have little hope of the blessing of heaven on our arms, if we insult it by our impiety and folly. Added to this, it is a vice so mean and low, without any temptation, that every man of sense and character detests and despises it."

It is unthinkable that we could consider the same high God we call on in prayer when we need Him now low enough to also use His name as a byword, dragging it through all kinds of filthy talking, and still expect Him to think we love and serve Him.

Christopher Morley, an American author of the early 1900s, once noted, "To many people the word 'God' is a formula on Sundays and an oath on weekdays."

God wants our respect (that's what the Bible means when it says "fear God") at all times. Close relationship between two parties is not possible unless each esteems the other continually and consistently.

The sacred loses its significance.

A man of my acquaintance had spent twenty years as a Navy Chaplain. He had so often used God's name in vain before becoming a Christian, that after making a commitment to Christ, he found himself unable to even use God's name in prayer, in worship, in song, or even in common conversation for a time. He had abused it so often.

Most of us at sometime in our childhood played a "King of the Mountain" game. While on a little hill, participants wrestled, shoved, and struggled to reach high ground and be the "King." It would mean nothing if the winner simply went to the hill when no one was there to push off. The game is in pushing others out of the way, using them to elevate one's self.

In taking God's name in vain, there is a similar principal involved. God is recognized as holding the "high ground." So if people wish to show how important they are, they "shove" God or Jesus off the high ground with profanity. In doing so they then have the euphoric feeling that they are now God, for they order God around and treat Christ like they command His destiny.

Washington Allston, a painter of the late 1700s, once wrote, "Reverence is an ennobling sentiment; it is felt to be degrading only by the vulgar mind, which would escape the sense of its own littleness by elevating itself into an antagonist of what is above it. He that has no pleasure in looking up is not fit so much as to look down."

Most swearing involves God, Jesus, or the sacred thing called motherhood. Why mothers? Many swear words are a disguised attack on them, because the process of bringing a new life, a brand new personality into existence is the one delegated act the God of all creation has given us. So when one swears using some term that casts aspersion on mothers, it is really a veiled attack on God.

But there are also words used in swearing without attacking God directly. When one would "damn" another individual, he is claiming he does not even need God to judge him. When one tells someone else he is full of some type of feces, he is denying another person's dignity and opposing the idea that "all men are created equal." He is deluding himself into thinking that he has almost a "divine" ability to order someone, by a burst of sudden exclamation, through the digestive tract of some animal and out through his bowels. This implies that he is nothing more than a glob of unused and unwanted chemical mass that smells worse than rotting food! It gives him a momentary high by stepping upon the dignity of another person in order to lift his own.

Someone has said, "Reverence is one of the signs of strength; irreverence one of the surest indications of weakness. No man will rise high who jeers at sacred things. The fine loyalties of life must be reverenced or they will be forsworn in the day of trial."

We try to manipulate God.

Some people pray to God, "Your will be done." What they really mean is, "God, I want You to approve my will."

In Psalm 8, we are told that human beings are made a "little lower than the heavenly beings" (v. 5). The word in the Hebrew here is *Elohim*, most often translated "God." If we translate it here as God, we are being told that we are God's highest creation next to himself. All else was created to serve us or be used by us for our maintenance, growth, and development. Only God is above us. Using profanity is a way of trying to manipulate God to do our own bidding, not His.

The same logic, the same process, is happening when we take God's name out of its sacred and holy context. It is an attempt to take over complete control of our life, and in this case we do it by elevating ourselves above God, an attempt to arrogate complete authority. We now feel we can manipulate God at will to do our bidding.

Let me illustrate what I mean. Have you ever heard someone say, "John damn you" or "Betty damn you"? No, because John, or Betty, or anybody else is on the same level or lower. The phrase used is always "God d— you." The person is saying, "I'm so big I can even tell God what to do. I'm ordering God to damn you."

Similarly when one wants to make an emphatic exclamation, it is not uncommon to hear "Jesus Christ." The one doing this could instead simply call out "Tom Brown" or "Mary Jones." But that would seem less dramatic, less impressive, less powerful. So the name of Jesus Christ is used. It's an effort to make a big impression by invoking the name of the Son of God whenever and wherever one wants.

In matters of common conversation, we need always to heed the admonition of Paul in Colossians 3:17: "Whatever you do, whether in word or deed, do it all in the name of the Lord Jesus, giving thanks to God the Father through him."

The Fourth VI Commandment

Remember the Sabbath day by keeping it holy (Exodus 20:8).

What Is the Background of the Commandment?

The division of time into a week of seven parts was not a Jewish invention. It seems rather to have originated in Babylon, where seven gods or spirits of the seven planets were each given a day.

At a much later time the Romans honored their gods Saturn, Apollo, Diana, Mars, Mercury, Jupiter, and Venus each with a day.

Even the English names for our days come from the names of the corresponding Scandinavian gods and goddesses. Wednesday was the day the god Woden was given attention; Thursday was the day the god Thor was worshiped. Sunday was the day the sun was honored.

In the days of the French Revolution, there was an effort to abolish everything that had to do with religion, and so they abolished a Sunday day of rest, substituting a ten day week. The experiment failed because the health of the nation was suffering.

Naturally, the delineation of the days of light and the nights of darkness come from the movement of our earth as it makes a complete revolution daily while making a yearly circle around our sun. By the time the Hebrews came into prominence, counting days and nights by seven was well established in societies. For them, as yet, one of the seven had not been designated as a special day.

The Scripture connects the Sabbath with God's creative activity at the beginning of all things. We are told He "blessed" and "made it holy" by setting it aside, because He "rested from all the work of creating . . ." (Genesis 2:3).

When the Jews were given manna in the Exodus, this commandment had not yet been revealed to Moses on Mt. Sinai. Each family was told to collect as much of this miraculous food that they needed each day. "On the sixth day, they gathered twice as much . . . for each person" (Exodus 16:22). Since earlier in the week, any manna kept overnight had spoiled, the leaders of the community reported to Moses what the people had done. He replied, "This is what the LORD commanded" (v. 23). The leaders had apparently not heard this instruction. The double amount gathered was necessary since the LORD did not give any manna on the Sabbath (v. 26). This was one way the people were to know the Sabbath was to be treated differently than other days. However, it seems likely that the Sabbath was in some way already an established special day, in that the first word introducing it in the book of Exodus is "Remember." Later, in Deuteronomy the Jews are admonished to "observe the Sabbath day by keeping it holy" (5:12), something that could not be done until after its clear recognition by the people.

Why Was This Commandment So Important?

Of all the Ten Commandments, this one is given the most stress. In terms of the amount of verses used to delineate it, there are four. The next in importance is the second proscribing idolatry, which is given three verses. This fact did not escape the Jews, for no laws were considered more important or more demanding than those that defined the Sabbath day and its proper observance. The Talmud stresses its value in relating that "two angels, one good, the other evil, accompanied every Jew on Sabbath eve from the synagogue to the house. If the Sabbath light is found lighted and the table spread, the good angel prays that this may be the case on the following Sabbath and the evil angel is compelled to say 'Amen' to this; but if no preparations for the Sabbath are seen, the evil angel pronounces a curse, and the good angel is compelled to say 'Amen'" (Shabbat 119b).

Further, the day was so weighty that it was considered "equal to all the other laws and commandments in the Torah," and that "whoever keeps the Sabbath holy is protected against temptation to sin" (Mekhilta 50b).

With respect to the nation as a whole, The Talmud says "if only two Sabbaths were properly observed, redemption would ensue at once. And if only one Sabbath was rightly kept, the Messiah would appear" (Shabbat 118b).

To the Jew, What Was Meant by "Rightly Kept"?

The most succinct account of why Israel was allowed to be plundered by enemies and taken into exile is given in 2 Kings 17. We are told that "the LORD warned Israel and Judah through all his prophets and seers: 'Turn from your evil ways. Observe my commands and decrees, in accordance with the entire Law. . . .'" But we are told that "they forsook all the commands of the LORD their God. . . . Therefore the LORD rejected all the people of Israel; . . . and gave them into the hands of plunderers, until he thrust them from his presence" (vv. 13, 16, 20).

The exile had a lasting impact on the Jews. Though they gained a semblance of independence when they returned, it did not last long. Through the centuries thereafter, the Jews were subjected to numerous conquests by their enemies. At times they also suffered severe containment. By conquest or by containment they were forced in upon themselves.

Because of the constant changing of their situation in the world, the Jews became fearful of change in their religion. The Sabbath suffered the most from the scribes' and Pharisees' attention, causing it to be changed from a day that protected the rights, health, and welfare of the working individual into an almost endless minutia of rules and regulations. This process continued between the Old and New Testaments. Fortunately, the synagogue was a strong institution. In some respects the worship it provided contributed more character to the Sabbath than the rules and regulations took from it.

The scribes and Pharisees began to give microscopic attention and word-splitting importance to every "jot and tittle" of God's revelation. They wanted to eliminate all gray areas. They desired to anticipate every thinkable situation that might happen to any individual. They sought to regulate every person's conduct to avoid in every way the possibility of any infraction that might lead to Sabbath desecration.

They searched the Scriptures for all indications of what was not to be done on the Sabbath. They turned their attention to the words of Jeremiah, who told the people, "This is what the LORD says: Be careful not to carry a load on the Sabbath day or bring it through the gates of Jerusalem. Do not bring a load out of your houses or do any work on the Sabbath, but keep the Sabbath day holy" (17:21-22).

The rabbis overlooked the fact that the prophet was likely referring to the people taking farm produce or home-manufactured articles to market on the Sabbath. They decided that carrying any load should be considered "work." They noted too that in connection with the manna instructions, the dictum translated literally was, "Let no man go out of his place" (Exodus 16:29, NASB). Did this mean one should not leave his place of abode on the Sabbath? To the observant Jew, the answer was "Yes!"

Numbers 35:5 indicates the limits of Levitical cities were three thousand feet from the city wall. Since the word "place" is used in the Hebrew in connection with the Cities of Refuge (Exodus 21:13), it was decided that the limits of such a city could be applied to a Sabbath journey. Thus, three thousand feet was considered the distance permissible for a Sabbath day's journey. (In Joshua 3:4 it is noteworthy that three thousand feet was also the distance allowed between the Ark and the people.)

Later, this three-thousand-foot limit posed a problem for those needing to go a greater distance. It was decided that if such a person went to the three thousand-foot mark before sunset on Friday and deposited a lunch, he could then come back to the place on the Sabbath. Eating the lunch would typify temporary residence, freeing him to go another three thousand feet without violating the Sabbath.

On the holiest day of the year, the Day of Atonement, a "scapegoat" had to carry the sins of the people into the wilderness. Since the wilderness area was several miles from Jerusalem, it was necessary to build a hut every three thousand feet to accommodate the person accompanying the goat so that he would not violate the Sabbath. Some Jews, such as the Essenes and the Samaritans, would hardly permit any movement on the Sabbath.

That such a distance was the restriction of movement on the Sabbath is recognized in Acts 1:12 where reference is made to "a Sabbath day's walk from the city."

Knowing that the law prohibited "work," the rabbis had to know "What is work?" They ultimately came up with 39 different classifications of what they called "fathers of work." A study of them indicates they were all connected with agricultural or home industry occupations. These were not considered sufficient to cover every situation involving work, so they expanded the 39 principals into as many as 1521 derivatives, arrived at by 39 x 39.

For example, since tying or untying a knot was considered work, it became necessary to determine what kind of knots were forbidden. It was decided that a knot which could not be untied with one hand was to be considered "labor" and thus forbidden on the Sabbath. Allowance had to be made, however, for any knot that was required in packing articles of food, or those that a woman might find necessary in getting dressed.

"Carrying a burden" was another of the 39 classes that had to be more carefully defined. What constituted a burden? Lifting a stone came under a ban. Then there was argument as to whether a parent lifting a child on the Sabbath was a burden. The child was deemed not a burden providing the child did not have a stone in his hand, for the stone would be a burden even if the child was not. That didn't end the discussion, however. The next question was "What constitutes a stone?"

To show how far some of the Jews took the definition of labor, the Essenes of the Dead Sea Scroll community refused to defecate or urinate on the Sabbath since this by law would require them to dig a hole, a prohibited act of labor on the Sabbath.

Matthew tells of the occasion of Jesus and the disciples going through a grain field on one Sabbath. The "disciples were hungry and began to pick some heads of grain and eat them" (12:1). The Pharisees complained that such was "reaping," and that was considered "work." Jesus responded that some things were necessary on the Sabbath, such as eating. He further told them "mercy" was more important than "sacrifice" (keeping the Sabbath law), and that He was "Lord of the Sabbath" (v. 8).

Soon after Jesus entered the synagogue, the Pharisees saw a man with a shriveled hand. Seeking to find cause to accuse Jesus, they asked Him if it was lawful to heal on the Sabbath. They held that it was not, for their law said one who was sick could only be kept from getting worse, but to make him get better was "work."

When Jesus completely restored his hand, the Pharisees began to plot His death.

The complaint the Pharisees had with Jesus healing the invalid at the pool of Bethesda (John 5) may not have been only that he, on orders from the Lord, was carrying his mat on the Sabbath or that he had walked too far. It may also have been that Jesus had used "magic" on the Sabbath to make him better.

Why Was the Commandment Given?

For humanitarian reasons.

It has been argued that this commandment was primarily a great piece of social and humanitarian legislation rather than a religious regulation. The day did have a practical side. It required rest from labor for everyone—men, women, and servants. Even toiling beasts were considered an integral part of the total community and needed to rest. The Bible required that land also was to experience a rest.

What would the world be without a Sabbath? According to Henry Ward Beecher, it "would be like a man without a smile, like a summer without flowers, and like a homestead without a garden. It is the most joyous day of the whole week."

To bring balance to life.

There is an old Greek proverb that states, "The bow that is always bent will soon cease to shoot straight." It is a rather accepted fact by those who study the technique of work, that efficiency diminishes in a worker as the week progresses. A day of rest restores that efficiency.

This is very apparent with the principal of the Sabbath. Yet in the second century before Christ, during Maccabean times, there were Jews who would stand and be killed in cold blood without the slightest attempt at defense if they were attacked on the Sabbath day. According to Josephus, the wily Roman general Pompey, knowing of the Jewish regard for the Sabbath, deliberately built a vast mound on the Sabbath from which to later attack Jerusalem. No resistance was encountered since the Jews were too fearful of breaking a Sabbath law. The Sabbath law had literally become dearer than life.

Now it is not difficult to understand why Jesus said, "The Sabbath was made for man, and not man for the Sabbath" (Mark 2:27). The Sabbath was intended to bring a balance to life, but the Jews caused it to become a day of imbalance.

In the words of Henry Wadsworth Longfellow, "Sunday is the golden clasp that binds together the volume of the week."

What Day Is to Be Remembered?

The Sabbath law was so strong that even first century Christians worshiped on the Sabbath. Since they were almost exclusively Jewish, the Sabbath law was binding. Yet to them there was another day that was of special significance. The Lord had risen on the first day of the week. It was but natural for this day to take on a greater and growing significance.

It is evident in the New Testament that the first day was already becoming a day of meaning. At the Council of Jerusalem, when consideration was being given to what would and would not be required of Gentile Christians, James recommended that Gentiles be required to "abstain from things contaminated by idols and from fornication and from [things] strangled, and from blood" (Acts 15:20 NASB). It is striking that there is no mention of observing the Sabbath.

In Genesis we are informed that "God blessed the seventh day and hallowed it, because on it God rested from all his work which he had done in creation" (2:3 RSV). Thus, for the Jew, the seventh day was the last day of a seven-day week.

It should be noted that Exodus 20:9-10 does not specify Saturday, nor the seventh day of the week, as the day for "rest." The emphasis is on the day that follows the six days of labor, whatever that day may be. Strictly speaking, even without the worship on Sunday because of Christ's resurrection on that day, in Old Testament understanding, Sunday fits the requirement just as much as does Saturday.

The demand by some that the Christian is to observe the Sabbath only on the seventh day of the week is, in effect, to place him under the law of the Old Testament. According to Exodus, a person would need to observe not gathering manna on the Sabbath (16:26) and not lighting a fire on that day (35:3). It was a violation of the Sabbath to gather sticks on this day (Numbers 15:33-35).

The Sabbath observance had become such a slavish thing to the early Christian church that Paul condemns those who observe days and months and seasons and years (Galatians 4:10; Colossians 2:16). He further affirmed that for one who is really strong in the faith there will be no special holy days at all, for all days are holy. While in theory this should be true, in practice we need a special day to refocus our attention from the necessary but mundane things of this world to our risen Lord.

The Sabbath day and the Lord's Day are different days and commemorate different events. The Sabbath is the last day of the week and commemorates God's rest after the toil of the week of creation; the Lord's Day is the first day of the week and commemorates the Resurrection of our Lord. It might be observed that the Sabbath is more of a backward-looking day; the Lord's Day is a forward-looking day, for those who honor it do so in the hope of the coming resurrection.

It was not humanly possible to maintain both a memorial to the creation, Saturday, and a memorial to the resurrection, Sunday. So slowly over about a century, the worship on the Lord's Day gained precedence and from the second century onward Sunday observances completely replaced Sabbath observances in the Christian communities.

Towards the close of the first century, by the time the book of Revelation was written, John talks of being "in the Spirit on the Lord's Day" (Revelation 1:10 NKJV).

How Does One Properly Remember?

Then one might ask what is the proper observance of the Lord's Day? How is one supposed to "remember it"?

By rest.

The word "Sabbath" comes from a Hebrew root meaning "to desist from work."

While the Scripture emphasizes that "God rested" on the seventh day, this was simply an exemplary rest. That is, He did not rest because He was tired, but He rested to show His creation what they were supposed to do.

Without going as far as did the Jews of intertestimental times, we need to define what is meant by "rest." When this commandment was given, nearly all work involved some type of strenuous physical activity. A man tilled the land with his oxen, reaped the harvest with backbreaking labor, or walked miles with his flock. By the end of the week every bone in his body ached. He was exhausted and physically drained. Rest for him was a time when he did nothing.

In today's society there is the segment of population termed "blue collar" whose work in production or assembly-line jobs requires a fair amount of physical activity. They are in greater need of "rest" than "white collar" activity which involves mainly sitting at a desk, or standing for periods of time, or sitting behind the wheel of a car. "Rest" for the "white collar" people should not be some kind of immobile activity, such as eating, sitting, or lying down. Such could put one on the fast track to a heart attack. For a body that has been relatively inactive, mixed with a mind that has had to be tense all week, "rest" may best be done by taking a hike, going for a swim, playing a game of golf or even mowing the lawn.

However, a Christian must always be mindful of what others may think about such activity on a Sunday, especially when there is available a Saturday, or another day of the week, for what might appear to the weaker believer to be "work."

But within the commandment is more than just "rest." It is evident the idea is to rest *from* work in order to be able to change our focus more directly *to* God, remembering His creative contribution to our lives.

By strengthening our families.

The family is under attack today by worldly forces. The authority of the parent is being undermined. Many youth are growing up rootless because of the loss of the family unit with a mother and a father. It was Henry Ward Beecher's observation that "we are not born as the partridge in the wood, or the ostrich of the desert, to be scattered everywhere; but we are to be grouped together, and brooded by love, and reared day by day in that first of churches, the family."

God put a heavy emphasis on the family. Commandments five and seven (honor of parents and sexual propriety) were directly aimed at the preservation of the family. And if we add the strengthening of families as a prominent end result of this one, it is safe to say 30% of the focus of the Ten Commandments is on the family. There is no religion today, nor has there ever been one, that sets a higher value on the family than Christianity.

In Old Testament times families lived, worked, slept, and did almost everything together. It was often the custom not to leave home when they married.

How vastly different it is in our society today. Many feel the economy requires both parents to have jobs away from home. It is not too uncommon for members of some families to scarcely see each other during the week. They eat few meals together and seldom even cross paths. If the people in Bible times needed a day of rest, we do all the more. For some, the Sunday noon meal can become a kind of sacrament of the family.

By encouraging fellowship.

The writer of Hebrews clearly saw the detriment that occurred when people become careless about church attendance when he wrote, "let us not give up meeting together, as some are in the habit of doing" (10:25).

At the height of his glory, Napoleon said, "I have courtiers; I don't need the fellowship of friends." How interesting! It was on a rocky little island where he spent the last years of his life—alone.

Henry Bellows, a prominent nineteenth-century clergyman, once observed, "I have never known a man, who habitually and on principle absented himself from the public worship of God, who did not sooner or later bring sorrow upon himself or his family."

By preserving sanctity.

The Scripture does not list the things one is to do in order to "remember," but as previously stated, it clearly implies one should "rest" *from* so that attention can be directed *to* God. Both are difficult, if not impossible, to do at the same time. Pursuit of legitimate secular and material goals is to be replaced with a day of necessary spiritual activity.

It goes without saying one cannot have a well-balanced personality without a shift of emphasis from the mundane, the secular, the earthly, to the spiritual dimension of the soul and the spirit—in short, to God.

William Jennings Bryan once observed that, "Man is a religious being; the heart instinctively seeks for a God. Whether he worships on the banks of the Ganges, prays with his face upturned to the sun, kneels toward Mecca or, regarding all space as a temple, communes with the Heavenly Father according to the Christian creed, man is essentially devout."

We were made to worship a higher being. It seems to me God put within all of us a space reserved exclusively for himself, and those who do not recognize it are never really fulfilled in life. They never really find meaning. They are destined to wander through life like vagabonds, always searching, never really finding. They try to fill that space with people, or money, or sex, or travel. Each of those substitutes is like trying to fit a square peg into a round hole.

It has been my observation that a person who does not revere God reveres little else about life. If there is no spiritual focus, then there is little respect, less courtesy, and insufficient reverence to give life the balance and meaning it needs. Virtues are wanting, values become confused, and life's normal flow is hindered. As reverence diminishes in the soul, vulgarity rises in proportion.

Hugh Blair was an eighteenth-century Scottish minister who believed, "It is for the sake of man, not of God, that worship and prayers are required; that man may be made better—that he may be confirmed in a proper sense of his dependent state, and acquire those pious and virtuous dispositions in which his highest improvement consists."

We might ask, "How can a day be holy?" It does not say that the *day* is to be holy, but that we are to *keep* the day holy. It appears that God wanted a special day set aside for maintaining and building up the spiritual life, a day when one withdraws from the common and dedicates himself to holy things.

Christ condemned a harshly defined day that expressed heartless delineation, but rather He emphasized its sacredness. He defined it as "for man's good" (Mark 2:23-28). Thus He stressed it was made not for God, but for people.

Read the words of St. Anselm. "Come now, little man! Flee for a while from your tasks, hide yourself for a little space from the turmoil of your thoughts. For a little while give your time to God, and rest in him for a little."

The biblical purpose of rest from work was desired by the LORD so His people would be better able to devote themselves to philosophy, contemplation, and improvement of character. It was to be a day for instruction. Aristobulus, successor to Philo, said the day should be "used for searching Scriptures, fostering the soul's power, searching after the knowledge of truth."

CHAPTER VII
The Fifth Commandment

Honor your father and your mother (Exodus 20:12).

Both the fifth and the seventh commandments are given to protect the family. The fifth is meant to emphasize the necessity of a quality internal structure. The seventh (not to commit adultery), is directed at external threats, encroachment from the outside.

As discussed in the preceding chapter, observing a day of rest is also meant to protect the family.

The Only Commandment with Promise

Throughout this book an effort is made to underscore the positive benefits that accrue to one who faithfully follows the commandments in daily life. But the fifth commandment is the only one that specifically states the benefit of the "lengthening of days," or long life.

It is normal to wonder how honoring parents can extend a life span. It would seem that in homes where there is more serenity and less stress, one develops more emotional stability. There is more respect for authority when children honor parents; when all things find a better balance in love, life is lengthened.

In his book, *Old Testament Law*, Dale Patrick writes, "Respecting and revering those who have gone before and on whom the individual depends forges a chain through history. The identity of the people is passed on to the next generation by the children's holding in reverence those who have embodied it."

Parents Were to Be Honored Equally

This commandment, as given in both Exodus 20:12 and Deuteronomy 5:16, puts the "father" in front of the "mother." In Leviticus 19:3, the word order is reversed. In the Hebrew language, word alignment is significant; the more important words were placed earlier in the sentence to give added emphasis.

The rabbis were meticulously interested in detail; they argued that both forms were given to ensure that the same honor was given to the mother as to the father.

It is safe to observe that no distinction was made between father and mother, for husband and wife are considered "one flesh." They are to be treated as equals.

Within the institutional structure of ancient Israel, men dominated the public institutions. But the family possessed an equality of sexes. The male heads of families were generally a part of the councils that made legal and political decisions. But women in the family unit exercised great influence. It is striking that at a time when society gave little opportunity for women to have positions of prominence or leadership, God repeatedly steers the people towards a greater recognition of women. A few of the more prominent examples include Deborah and Esther in leadership roles, and Rahab, Jael, and Ruth in very crucial circumstances.

The family, then and now, derives its existence from the interaction of male and female. Both parties are to receive the honor due those responsible for the family's existence and maintenance.

This Commandment Suffered Much Abuse

The problem of *korban*.

In order to avoid helping their fathers and mothers, some people would subtly evoke God's commandment in Leviticus 1:2 to set apart an offering [korban] for God alone. Jesus condemned this action in Mark 7:9-13 when he said, "For Moses said, 'Honor your father and your mother.' . . . But you say that if a man says to his father and mother: 'Whatever help you might otherwise have received from me is Korban' (that is, a gift devoted to God), then you no longer let him do anything for his father or mother." Honoring one's father and mother is not an option here.

The problem of commensurate punishment.

Jesus reiterated the importance of this commandment when He said, "God commanded saying, . . . he who curses father or mother let him be put to death" (Matthew 15:4 NKJV).

The Old Testament law specified the death penalty for "striking" or "cursing" a parent (Exodus 21:15, 17; Leviticus 20:9). Incorrigibility also was thought to merit surrendering one's life (Deuteronomy 21:18-21).

Forms of punishment necessarily have always had to conform to the cultural expression of the time—in this case it was stoning. It was not possible to punish by lethal injection or electrocution. Stoning was the acceptable and, at that time thought to be, the most humane punishment. One imagines that the punishment, so severe, made people give more recognition to the law and more care to respect it.

Stoning is not practiced now. Few, if any, today would advocate death for a child's incorrigibility. Yet God's main concern now, as then, is to ensure respect for the authority of parents over children and for honor of parents by the children.

What does honor require?

For children, depending on age, honor means dependence, then obedience, then respect.

Some have thought that this was the one commandment included to make sure children were not forgotten and were covered in the law. But while honor necessarily includes obedience, obedience diminishes with age. This commandment goes far beyond that.

For adults, honor involves love, then respect, and eventually caring for their parents. Children should help maintain their parents' dignity even when they, because of age, move into a state of dependence.

The Hebrew word for "honor" is frequently used with God as the object. Wherever it is used that way it is translated "glorify." To honor parents then is to accord them a respect and importance reserved for the sacred.

More attention should be given to Jesus' example. He spent over ninety percent of His thirty-three years in His village home. Joseph may have died early—he is not mentioned at the wedding of Cana. Being the eldest son, Jesus likely had to take care of His mother and younger brothers and sisters. And He was still thinking of His mother as He hung on the cross, finally committing her to the care of John.

Honor includes obedience and love.

The apostle Paul admonished, "Children, obey your parents in the Lord, for it is right" (Ephesians 6:1). Of necessity, this must be tempered by two things: the child's age, and the morality of the command.

No one expects a person of thirty or forty years of age to obey father and mother. However, no one can ever escape the command to honor parents, even after their death.

But with respect to the morality of the command, should a child be expected to obey an order to do evil? The "obey" here is qualified by "in the Lord." Parents are to be shown honor, but nowhere are their words, or wishes, to become a rival or a substitute for the will or Word of God. Parents are to love their children for this too is right in the Lord. A parent who loves will never ask a child to do anything contrary to the child's good.

It is important to recognize that biblical truth is always a reciprocal truth. It never lays all the duty on one side. There is always an equal duty on the other.

An example of this is given of Jesus' "turn-the-other-cheek" statement in Matthew 5:39. We are provided a record in John 18:19-23 of Jesus being interrogated by Annas, father-in-law of Caiaphas, the high priest. Dissatisfied with the reply Jesus gave, a servant of the high priest slapped Him on the cheek. Jesus' response gives us His interpretation of what He meant by His "cheek" statement. "If I said something wrong, . . . testify as to what is wrong. But if I spoke the truth, why did you strike me?" Jesus did not react in kind, but rather made the man come face-to-face with the responsibility of his act.

There is a sense in which parents must earn the right to be obeyed. It is entirely possible that many Christian parents have not earned that right. A dictator or a tyrant parent may demand obedience, but he most likely has not earned it by tempering it with love. Discipline must be seasoned with love.

This was demonstrated to me when my daughter of nine months of age was being entertained by her eight-year-old sister. Suddenly the joyous laughter was replaced with a cry of pain.

Rushing into the room, I began quizzing the older daughter on what she had done. "Did you pinch?" "No!" "Did you twist her arm?" "No!" "Did you sit on her?" "No!" Finally, I asked, "Did you bite her?" Same "No!" reply. I had asked the question knowing in the past there had been playful biting sometimes.

Upending the baby to look for perhaps an undone safety pin, I saw the telltale red teeth marks of the older daughter's bite. I responded, "You lied to me!"

She was given a spanking and sent to bed. I had disciplined, but as yet not loved enough. After a few minutes of sobbing, I entered the room, knelt down, and touching my head to hers, I said, "Honey, I love you. Do you understand why I punished you?" The reply was, "Yes, because I bit sister." "No. No." I quickly answered, "Not because you bit your sister, but because you lied to me. I must teach you to always be truthful."

The point is, my daughter would have misunderstood the reason for the discipline if I had not seasoned it with love.

Parents must realize they are the pattern that sets in the mind of a child what God is like, for the father and mother are the master teachers of the child.

I recall during a spiritual emphasis service one fall semester, I sought to help a young first year coed kneeling at the altar. After asking her name, I inquired of her purpose for coming forward. She told me she wanted to understand God better. I quickly responded, "It's really simple! Just think of God as a loving father. . . ." Immediately interrupting me, and pushing herself back from the altar, she responded, "Don't say that! Don't compare God to my father! He hates me! He abused me. He kicked me out of the house! Don't compare God to my father!"

Not having had such a reaction before, I immediately asked God for help. Then I replied, "Well, look at it this way. What your father was not and should have been, God is!" In this way I helped her work through her difficulty.

Four years later I again found the same young lady at the altar. This time when I asked the cause of her response in the service, she replied, "I am doing my practice teaching now, and I love the children so much. I just want God to help me love them more."

Chuckling a bit, I asked, "Do you recall four years ago you bowed at this altar and had a great difficulty understanding love because of the way your father had treated you? Now you understand what love truly is, and you want more of it!"

Parents who do not properly love their children when disciplining them help to create a void in properly understanding God and properly relating to Him.

It is little wonder why a child who has been physically, emotionally, or sexually abused by a parent has much greater difficulty understanding God as a heavenly Father who loves His children and only wants what is best for them.

The Hebrews recognized this fact. The word for parents is *horim*, which comes from the same root as the word for teacher, *moreh*. The parent is, and remains, the first and most important teacher that the child will ever have.

Paul said, "Fathers, do not exasperate your children; instead, bring them up in the training and instruction of the Lord" (Ephesians 6:4).

Honor includes respect and gratitude.

Of wisdom, Proverbs 4:8 says, "Esteem her, and she will exalt you; embrace her, and she will honor you." To esteem is to "prize highly."

A child owes his life to his parents: his birth, his care, and his provision when the child could not provide for himself. It is striking how different we humans are from animals. Most offspring of animals have to learn to walk before they can eat. This is not so with human babies. They are born almost totally helpless. It would seem that God said, "I want the human family to be different. I want to put a bundle of human flesh where it will be guided by law, tempered by love, and learn respect and gratitude."

Honor includes affection and care.

When children are grown, they must see that their parents do not lack for the necessities of life and that they are not left in need or in loneliness. It is not uncommon in our day for children to virtually abandon their parents in nursing homes and senior care facilities. Sometimes such institutions are the best place for parents, especially if they need specialized care, but there is no excuse for children to ignore them during their period of need. To do so is only to invite the same attitude toward themselves when the children are in a similar situation.

This does not necessarily mean children should immediately bring parents to their home. All aged people have a right to, and should be entitled to, a home of their own as long as they are physically and emotionally able to have one.

Some years ago it became evident to me that my parents were going to need increased supervision. Not wanting to cheat them out of their own independence any more than necessary, I purchased a house in my town within a few blocks of my own. With daily visits to make sure their needs were being met, I was able to extend their independence for five years until it became necessary for them to have more supervised care.

During those years I visited them once, at times twice, a day. When that was not possible because of my schedule, my wife or one of my children would take my place.

Later more specialized care was needed than I could give. They moved to a facility that was approximately fifty miles away. I made the trip weekly, each time taking my teen-aged daughters with me. I wanted them to know I cared for my parents, their best interests, and did not want to slight them. My mother outlived my father by two years. At 82 years of age, she did not recognize us any more. We visited anyway. Was it worth the effort? I answer with a resounding yes! After she passed on, my daughters went to a local nursing home and "adopted" another grandmother to visit weekly. Need I say that as I age, and ultimately need more care, I will have put currency "in the bank" so to speak, the account of which my daughters will draw upon. This illustrates my next point.

How Does This Commandment Carry Its Own Punishment?

The one who violates this commandment will be haunted by it in at least two ways.

We receive what we give.

We cut a groove in our children by the way we regard our own parents. This book was begun during those years when my parents became my wards in that I had to look after them. During a period when my mother developed cancer, the doctor, unsure of the success of impending surgery, advised me to get power of attorney for them.

From that time I decided to keep my parents' money in a separate account. On one occasion I needed $200, an amount that exceeded my means. While deciding what to do, I was tempted to simply take the money from their account. The temptation pressure was emboldened with the thought, "They will never know."

Having recently come upon the theory that the commandments never state punishments for their violation because the punishment was built within the infraction, I asked myself, "How will I hurt myself if I take what will likely at some time come to me anyway?"

Almost immediately it seemed the Lord put into my mind the thought of my three daughters. "There it is!" I concluded, "All I have to do is return home and say to my wife, 'I know where I can get the money I need. My old folks won't know. I'll just take it from their account.'" In a very few years that decision would come back to haunt me. I will be in the place of my parents and my daughters will think, "Well, that's the way he treated his parents, so I guess that's the way we will treat him."

The Greek philosopher Euripides observed, "Unblessed is the son who does not honor his parents; but if reverent and obedient to them, he will receive the same from his own children."

All of us are children of parents and our obligation does not cease as long as they live and it should continue on after they die. By showing honor to our parents we strengthen the system that bestows honor on ourselves as parents.

In a book entitled *You and Your Aging Parents* is found a folk tale that stresses this point.

An ancient grandmother lived with her daughter and grandson. As she grew frail and feeble, instead of being a help around the house, she became a constant trial. She broke plates and cups, lost knives and spilled water. One day, exasperated because the old woman had broken another precious plate, the daughter sent the grandson to buy his grandmother a wooden plate.

The boy hesitated because he knew a wooden plate would humiliate his grandmother. But his mother insisted, so off he went. He returned bringing not one, but two wooden plates.

"I only asked you to buy one," his mother said. "Didn't you hear me?"

"Yes," said the boy. "But I bought the second one so there would be one for you when you get old."

Some years ago a very prominent businessman moved his wife's parents to my city. He needed a place for them to live. I happened to have a mobile home available. He rented it for them. Some time later I mentioned to him how glad I was that I had the residence available; it had worked so well for my parents for a few years.

His reply was, "Well, I'd like to lock the door on them and throw the key away! They don't deserve any attention after the way they treated me when I wanted to marry their daughter!"

Mentioning his six-year-old son standing nearby, I called him by name and asked, "Do you realize you are infecting the atmosphere of your life with that attitude toward those parents? It is no doubt being registered on the minds of your children, and in a few years it could come back to haunt you."

From that time on, I never heard him speak the same way about his in-laws. I think he had just not looked ahead enough to see that what he was giving would eventually come back to him.

May Maldo has written, "Children seldom misquote you. They more often repeat word for word what you shouldn't have said."

We give birth to what we are.

Olivia de Havilland once said, "I am convinced one has a tendency to repeat the emotional errors of one's parents. If one is the product of divorced parents, or inharmoniously married parents—it's not whether they stay together or not, but what their conflicts are that counts—you are apt to copy, quite unconsciously, their pattern."

A daughter who has difficulty relating to a father may very probably become a wife who has difficulty relating properly to her husband.

A son who won't appreciate his mother should not wonder why he later has difficulty relating properly to his wife.

If we permit a gap to separate us from our parents, we may soon find ourselves on the other side of a gap between our own children and us.

A young teenager who *will not* understand his own parents is more likely to become a parent who *cannot* understand his own children.

The philosopher John Locke once wrote "Parents wonder why the streams are bitter when they themselves have poisoned the fountain."

The number one killer of children under five is not cancer, not disease, not crib death, not accident; it is child abuse. Surprisingly, the majority of that group, 67 percent, occurs to children under four. A full third of that number is of abuse to children less than six months of age.

Consider also that abused children almost invariably grow up to become parents who abuse their own children. Perhaps to "get even," they may also abuse their older and helpless parents.

"When thou art contemplating some base deed, let the presence of thy infant son act as a check on thy headlong course to sin"—Juvenal.

One teen said to another, "No wonder Monette gets straight A's in French.

Her parents were born in Paris and speak French at home."

Said the listening teen, "In that case I ought to get A's in geometry. My parents are square and talk in circles."

The comedian Sam Levenson said, "Insanity is hereditary. You can get it from your children."

A house may be said to have its own atmosphere. Children raised in it breathe in that climate every day. It has been aptly said:

If a child lives with criticism, he learns to condemn.
If a child lives with hostility, he learns to fight.
If a child lives with fear, he learns to be apprehensive.
If a child lives with jealousy, he learns to feel guilty.
If a child lives with tolerance, he learns to be patient.
If a child lives with encouragement, he learns to be confident.
If a child lives with praise, he learns to be appreciative.
If a child lives with acceptance, he learns to love.
If a child lives with approval, he learns to like himself.
If a child lives with recognition, he learns it is good to have a goal.
If a child lives with honesty, he learns what truth is.
If a child lives with fairness, he learns justice.
If a child lives with security, he learns to have faith in himself and those about him.
If a child lives with friendliness, he learns the world is a nice place in which to live.

Carl Menninger, the noted psychiatrist, said, "What is done to children, they will do to society."

Sociobiology is a study that emerged in the 1980s. It is a mixture of the disciplines of biology, sociology, and psychology. It is the study of the biological factors on behavior. In this field, recent studies are pointing to the connection of the genetic effect between parents and children relating to their behavior, good or bad.

There is an undeniable power of mind over matter. Undue stress on the body can cause shingles or stomach ulcers. Anger or fear in any given situation can make it most difficult for a person to act normally.

Environmental factors are pervasive. But a greater recognition is now being given to the influence of genetic factors in behavior.

Edward O. Wilson of Harvard University was one of the main exponents of this discipline. In his book, *Sociobiology, the New Synthesis*, he wrote, "Sociobiology is leading to the view of man as being under the influence of

77

inherited programs of behavior that are more strict than many psychologists would have us believe."

In other words, we act as we act in degree, less according to our environment and more according to what we inherited from our parents than was formerly thought.

With regard to the second commandment, the LORD says, "I, the LORD your God, am a jealous God, punishing the children for the sin of the fathers to the third and fourth generation of those who hate me, but showing love to thousands who love me and keep my commandments" (Exodus 20:5-6).

The mark of Adam and Eve is on us all genetically. Of this there is no doubt.

Children of artists often have a greater innate capacity for artistic expression. Parents who are musicians often have children who have a greater capacity for music. Exposure to the environment of art and music can have an encouraging effect, but the capacity must first be there.

Here are some penetrating questions to consider: What about one's capacity for evil? Or the capacity for good? Are these governed somewhat by what parents pass on to their children? Does a child conceived in sin have a greater capacity for evil than one conceived by godly parents? Such questions cannot be answered with absolute certainty. Yet it seems a given that the environmentally-influenced generation is the second generation. The third and fourth generations point more to genetic influences.

The Sixth Commandment

You shall not kill (Exodus 20:13 RSV).

There are those today that use this commandment to oppose the taking of human life in capital punishment. There are others who believe the injunction is against the taking of any life, even that of animals, and therefore they oppose even the consumption of any meat.

The Biblical Meaning of Kill

The commandment does not say, "you shall not kill" in the sense that the word is most commonly used. The Hebrew verb implies a violent and unauthorized killing. If this commandment included the killing of all things, even animals, then God would be holding a double standard. He is telling people not to kill on the one hand and on the other mandating a system of sacrifices that required the killing of animals. God instituted sacrifices to atone for sin and as a way to maintain fellowship and communion with God himself.

The intent of the commandment is rather "You shall not murder." It is not possible for us to "murder" a cow, or a rabbit, or even a bird, because in the God-ordained hierarchy of life, they are beneath us. The hierarchy of human life is predicated on the fact that taking life "down" is not murder. Furthermore, for us to murder "up" is impossible, for the only thing above us is God himself and we cannot kill Him. But killing *laterally* or "sideways" is murder, if it is unauthorized and violent.

Is the killing of a person ever justified, even when social justice or legitimate punishment is the consideration?

The unauthorized taking of the life of one who is guilty of murdering another individual, in biblical understanding, does violate this commandment. However, judicial killing is never considered murder in the Bible.

When the statement is made in Exodus 21:24, "life for life, eye for eye, tooth for tooth," the proper understanding of the statement is, "let the punishment be commensurate with the deed committed," or "let the punishment fit the crime."

In support of this viewpoint, Exodus 21:12 makes it clear that a life is to be surrendered only when there is the intentional killing of a person.

In Leviticus 24:17, the Hebrew verb "smites" legislates that the one who intentionally kills another person shall pay with his own life. But "anyone who takes the life of [kills] someone's animal must make restitution—life for life" (v. 18). The one who committed the infraction shall pay for it with a like animal.

Notice how the Apostle Paul looked at this matter of punishment. He had been framed and accused by the Jews successfully. And they, wanting to see him killed, got him tried before Festus. This Roman official wanted to do the Jews a favor, so he was seeking for a cause to punish Paul. After declaring his innocence (Acts 25:10), Paul then recognizes the legitimacy of the death penalty in the next verse when he says, "If, however, I am guilty of doing anything deserving death, I do not refuse to die" (v. 11).

Paul quotes Deuteronomy 32:35, when he writes, "Never take your own revenge . . . leave room for the wrath of God, for it is written, 'Vengeance is mine, I will repay'" (Romans 12:19 NASB).

The intent of this passage is to emphasize that God will settle accounts in the judgment. But this does not mean that a judicial body, chosen by the people should not exact the maximum punishment of surrendering one's life if he has been guilty of taking that of another in a violent manner.

In Romans 13:4, Paul recognized the need for being in subjection to rulers vested with the right to exercise authority. So did Peter when he wrote concerning supreme authority, "submit yourselves to those who are sent by him [God] to punish those who do wrong . . ." (1 Peter 2:13-14).

In His teaching in the Sermon on the Mount, Jesus said, "You have heard that it was said, 'an eye for an eye, and a tooth for a tooth.' But I say to you, do not resist him who is evil; but whoever slaps you on your right cheek, turn to him the other also" (Matthew 5:38-39 NASB). Here the Lord is not abrogating the Old Testament commandment of an "eye for an eye, and tooth for tooth," and replacing it. He is rather speaking with respect to the attitude of the common individual who should not have retribution in mind.

The Pharisaical approach of Christ's day was to disregard one's personal attitude with respect to any and all laws. Jesus emphasized their importance, and He made what one thought always applicable. One was guilty of adultery even though the person had only gone as far as lusting (Matthew 5:28).

What Makes Murder So Wrong?

The Old Testament presents life as created and existing "in the image of God," and is therefore considered sacred. If life is sacred, it is then precious. And what is precious is of great value.

When one takes the life of another it is really an attempt to "play God," to decide who stays in this life and who doesn't. It is reversing the God-ordained roles. Animals were given to "serve us," so to speak. They were to provide us with food. We were never intended to "serve animals." An animal that caused the death of another person was to be put to death (Exodus 21:28-32).

We were created to serve God. God is not to serve us, though many try to make Him do that. We are to serve each other. For me to kill another individual is to treat him as though he was intended to serve my purposes.

It is also usurping God's place. To kill a person is tantamount to killing God in effigy, for all humans have God's image.

What Were the Prescribed Crimes for Which the Death Penalty Was Applied?

In reality the death penalty was enforced for many and varied crimes besides murder. A life was taken for certain religious and ritual offenses, such as witchcraft, idolatry, blasphemy, false prophecy, intrusion by an alien into a sacred place or a sacred office, and breaking or profaning the Sabbath.

A man's life was required if he kept an ox known to be dangerous (if the ox had gored someone), lying in a capital charge, kidnapping, incorrigible delinquency (that is, insult or injury to parents and authorities), offering human sacrifice or sacrificing to false gods, and practicing magic or divination.

Then there was a whole class of sexual promiscuity situations that required the death penalty. This list included adultery, homosexuality, sex with a family member (incest), or with an animal, unchastity, and fornication with an engaged woman. The means used for judicial punishment were stoning, burning, beheading, and strangling.

How Did These Laws Compare with Other Laws of Their Time?

It is interesting to note that other contemporary laws of the day prescribed capital punishment in similar manner to that of the Bible. The one exception was trial by ordeal. But it was also common for society to punish for crimes against property. In the Old Testament no crime against property warranted the death of the guilty person. The biblical point of view was, and is, that *things* were not sacred; *life* is. Anything that aimed at destroying the sacred quality of life was a capital offense against God.

So sacred was life that all violent forms of snatching it away caused guilt to fall upon the land and had to lead to the yielding of another life. Only in the case of premeditated murder was a "ransom" or a "substitute" payment unacceptable (Numbers 35:31), but presumably all the other capital crimes could be commuted if the judges so determined. The death penalty was to underscore the seriousness of these errors.

Accidental homicide or manslaughter was, and today is, distinguished from calculated and deliberate murder.

Included in legislation was the warning about dangerous animals (Exodus 21:29, 36), the need for parapets around roofs to prevent people from falling off (Deuteronomy 22:8), and digging pits without covers that might cause men or animals to fall into them (Exodus 21:33-34).

Was the Death Penalty Often Carried Out?

While Old Testament law did provide for the death penalty, it also made it very difficult to carry out.

The various laws concerning the death penalty show the seriousness with which these sins were regarded, but the administration of the law indicates that mercy was shown to the sinner. Indeed, there was a certain sternness in Old Testament law, but shrouding it was a certain leniency with regard to the one who had broken it.

According to Deuteronomy 17:6 and Numbers 35:30, no one could be condemned on any evidence less than that of two eyewitnesses. Any evidence not based on such verification carried little validity in a Jewish court.

The intent of this legislation, according to the best Jewish minds of biblical times, was that one could not have his life taken unless two eyewitnesses who were "qualified" saw his crime. Furthermore, they must be of legal age, have a sound mind, have acted without the aid of others, and the one accused must have been forewarned of the consequences of his deed before he acted. Additionally, one was not considered guilty until all these limitations had been satisfied. The guilty person was to have the death sentence carried out on the same day of the conviction.

Since even the criminal was considered a brother to be loved (Leviticus 19:18), that spirit had to be manifested. This was done by intentionally locating the place of execution outside the town where the trial took place. As the convicted was slowly led towards his place of destiny, a herald preceded him loudly inviting anyone who had any evidence favorable to the doomed man to immediately step forward and reveal it. The judges remained in session all day, fasting the whole time, in the event more evidence was disclosed after the trial had ended. If evidence was forthcoming, a horse-mounted rider would stop the procession, turn it around, and lead it back to the court so the new information would be considered.

It is clear that while capital punishment was enacted, every effort was made to reduce its practice to a minimum, but not to eliminate it altogether. They may well have felt like Daniel Webster centuries later who observed, "Every unpunished murder takes away something from the security of every man's life."

This is clearly underscored with regard to the killing of a person. The priests of the tribe of Levi were to be the religious servants of the country. Instead of being given land as a tribal inheritance, they were awarded 48 cities somewhat equally distributed throughout the other tribal allotments, which was an average of four to a tribe. (Ephraim and Manasseh were both sons of Joseph who received his "double portion," thus returning the tribal number to 12 of those who were to receive an allotment of land.)

To make sure the death penalty was administered fairly, six of these cities were called "Cities of Refuge." Three of them were located east of the Jordan River, and three west of it. Of these six cities, two were in the north, two in the center, two in the south and all somewhat evenly distributed geographically so that no one would be living more than thirty-some miles away from any one city. The pre-biblical law allowed for anyone who had killed another person to have justice exacted by a member of the aggrieved family. That person was called the "avenger."

Biblical law provided that if death had resulted from some incident or accident, the person accused could flee to one of the six cities of refuge, and thus escape the avenger who would most certainly be too biased to act with justice. This appointed city of refuge only gave him temporary safety and asylum from the avenger until an investigation into the crime could be made. As stated earlier, the trial did not allow for one to be convicted on the testimony of only one witness. If the trial determined that the killing was intentional, the guilty one would be handed over to the avenger, who no doubt was near the city gate awaiting the outcome of the investigation, or the elders of the city of refuge would sentence him to death.

If the investigation proved that the killing was accidental, the guilty one was to remain in his city of refuge until the serving high priest died, after which he was considered to have paid his penalty. And if the blood avenger killed him, then the blood avenger would be required to stand trial for intentional murder.

It would appear that the "eye for eye, tooth for tooth" legislation had been interpreted in such a way as to cause blood feuds to develop, causing the law to be interpreted literally. Desiring to restore the correct interpretation of this law, these six cities were established so that a fair system of justice could be administered.

How Does This Commandment Relate to the Problem of Capital Punishment Today?

The real reason for this commandment is stated succinctly in God's statement to Noah after the flood. "And for your lifeblood I will surely demand an accounting. I will demand an accounting from every animal. And from each man, too, I will demand an accounting for the life of his fellow man" (Genesis 9:5-6).

It would appear that God is telling us that we not only have the capacity, but the obligation to take the life of anything or any creature that presumes to kill a human being, thus eliminating one of God's ambassadors on earth.

Notice the words of Paul, "If you do what is evil, be afraid; for it [authority] does not bear the sword for nothing; for it is a minister of God, an avenger who brings wrath upon the one who practices evil" (Romans 13:4 NASB). The words of Peter are also significant. "Submit yourselves for the Lord's sake to every human institution, whether to a king as the one in authority; or to governors as sent by him for the punishment of evildoers" (1 Peter 2:13-14 NASB). The implication is that a government has the right to execute punishment where such punishment is in conformity with biblical principles.

"Killing, when permitted or even commanded, is to be regarded as in principle a consequence of the duty of the preservation of life in the higher sense"—John P. Lange.

How Does This Commandment Relate to the Problem of Euthanasia?

Euthanasia is the belief that when a person's life has become unlivable to himself, and when that life is worse than death, then that life may be legitimately taken away. This is a growing phenomenon in our day.

According to this belief, a person who is suffering from some incurable and agonizing disease might be killed kindly, humanely, and presumably with his own consent, if he is still able to give consent. Or those who hold this belief might argue that a child born deformed and obviously quite unable ever to live in the real sense might never be allowed to grow up. Or, it might be held, a child incurably mentally deficient might be deprived of life before life ever really begins.

There is great difficulty in defining the area in which euthanasia might be practiced.

Just when does a person reach that stage when it would be better for him or her to have life ended? How is the word *incurable* to be defined? Is it not the case that many diseases that were once incurable are curable now? What guarantee is there that a disease that is incurable at the present moment may not become curable within the lifetime of the person who has it?

(1) Who would make the decision for ending a person's life?

Would the relatives have the say? Would the person's own doctor decide? Would there be some special panel or commission that would investigate each case and then decide? What part in the decision would the person himself have? The responsibility for decision would present intolerable problems.

(2) Who would be responsible for carrying out the decision?

Who would carry out what in law was a kind of justifiable homicide? This obviously could not be left in the hands of the individual. The medical profession would clearly refuse the responsibility as well. It would be intolerable that there should be a kind of public "executioner." To saddle anyone with that kind of responsibility would be an impossibility.

Any such scheme would lend itself to enormous abuse.

Once the right to take life is allowed under any circumstances, the circumstances may at anytime be fabricated or unduly extended. The way would be open for the extermination of the aged and the infirm. A whole class of unwanted citizens could be eliminated, as happened in Hitler's Germany, or more recently in the Balkans. The operation of the scheme would involve and require such complicated safeguards and such unceasing vigilance that it would become impossible.

The biblical position clearly says it is basically wrong to give any one person the power of life and death.

What Is the Christian Attitude Toward Suicide?

Anything said about this subject must take into account the practices in the Bible. The first who is recorded as having died by his own instruction was Abimelech, one of the seventy sons of the judge Gideon. Knowing his father had refused the peoples' request for him to be their king, Abimelech decided he would take advantage of the request, though he knew it did not involve him (Judges 8:22-35). He gained the support of his mother's people at Shechem, even receiving seventy shekel weights of silver. (If the price Micah offered the Levite in Judges 17:10, "ten shekels of silver a year," represented a typical annual wage at that time, the sum of seventy shekel weights was sizable.) Though it was intended for a pagan temple, Abimelech instead used the silver to hire "reckless adventurers" to follow him.

Abimelech then proceeded to kill all his brothers except one, to keep them from challenging his move (Judges 9:1-6). When a woman cracked his skull by dropping a stone on his head, he called on his armor-bearer to kill him. He did not want it to be said that a woman had killed him (Judges 9:50-57). His case certainly is not in the Bible as an example to follow.

Another biblical case is that of King Saul who was wounded and wanted his armor bearer to kill him, "lest these uncircumcised come and pierce me through and make sport of me" (1 Samuel 31:4-6 NASB). After the attendant refused, Saul fell on his own sword, committing suicide.

We also learn of Ahithophel, a crafty but sinister advisor of King David who cast his lot with Absalom, a rebellious son of David. Through the LORD's prompting, David asked one of his old, but trusted, advisors, Hushai, to return to Jerusalem to pretend to be loyal to Absalom, but to counter the advise of Ahithophel. It worked. Then we are told, "When Ahithophel saw that his counsel was not followed, he saddled his donkey and arose and went to his home, to his city, and set his house in order, and strangled himself; thus he died and was buried in the grave of his father" (2 Samuel 17:23).

First Kings 16:18 records the act of Zimri, a chariot commander of King Elah, who murdered him in an effort to take over the monarchy. This occurred after only seven days on the throne. When the army learned what had happened, they installed Omri as king. An attack was made on the capital. When Zimri learned of it, he set fire to the palace and perished in the flames.

In the case of both Ahithophel and Zimri, neither could be considered a man who was following the LORD. Saul too, by his own testimony to Samuel, admitted, "God has departed from me and answers me no more" (1 Samuel 28:15 NASB). In no way could the acts of these men be considered justified. In this author's opinion, suicide for whatever reason, is self-murder.

The Seventh Commandment

You shall not commit adultery (Exodus 20:14).

A rather well-known comedian a few years ago said, "TV has come a long way, baby. Sex, violence, profanity, drugs, nudity—it's all acceptable now on TV—as long as they don't smoke cigarettes."

In our lifetime we have witnessed a raising of health standards, improved nutrition, refined medications, and thereby have lengthened life spans, but we are actually losing ground in improving our moral health. Why is this so? More than any other reason, it is an increasing disregard for this seventh commandment.

Six Questions to Help Us Understand Why This Prohibition Is Found Among the Ten Commandments

What is the meaning of this commandment?

The dictionary definition of adultery is "voluntary sexual intercourse between a married man and someone other than his wife, or between a married woman and someone other than her husband."

Then one might ask, "Since the Bible says nothing about premarital sex, is it really wrong?" Why not argue as do some teenagers today: "I get hunger pains, and I don't have to wait for an 'I do' to satisfy them. Why do I have to wait to use my sexual drives?"

Premarital sex was not a problem in biblical times. If it had been, the Bible would be more specific about it. By the same argument, smoking was not known in biblical times, so why all the arguments against it now? The Bible dealt with problems that existed at the time of its writing. But it also gave rules of conduct that could be applied at any time in any place.

The thrust of this commandment is "Don't take sex out of its God-intended limits." God created sex to be very good inside the limitation of marriage. Outside of those limits it can be damaging physically, morally, and spiritually.

Marriage was important to God. Jesus began His ministry at a wedding at Cana in Galilee (John 2). He will conclude His ministry in heaven with what John called the "marriage supper of the Lamb" (Revelation 19:9 NASB).

What were, and what are, God's intended limits?

The biblical view of moral integrity is summed up in Joseph's view of illicit sex when Potiphar's wife tried to seduce him. He called it a "sin against God." He said, "How then can I do this great wickedness and sin against God?" (Genesis 39:9 NKJV).

David was repenting for the sin of adultery with Bathsheba and the murder of her husband, Uriah, as he wrote Psalm 51. In it he said "Against you, you only, have I sinned and done what is evil in your sight" (v. 4).

Very early in Genesis, God gave the ideal blend in monogamous relationships. "A man will leave his father and mother and be united to his wife, and they will become one flesh" (2:24). To have multiple wives was a pagan practice to emphasize influence and affluence. The pages of the Word shows how the people who practiced it brought a limitation to their own contentment.

What did God have in mind when He said, "The two shall become one flesh"?

The ideal of one wife for one man is also emphasized in Proverbs 5:15-19. Tactfully, but clearly, the figure of speech is given that drinking from one's own water source was to be reserved for one person "alone, never to be shared with strangers" (v. 17). Sex was not to be put on the street! In the Song of Solomon, where the purposes, joys, and sanctity of marriage are underscored, couples are urged to delight in each other's love and beauty.

There is a type of physical oneness that is attained when a man and a woman come together sexually, but that only underscores an emotional and psychological union of the spirit that God also wanted to occur. For one member of that union to try to include another on the side is as destructive to that oneness as it is to the worship of the one God when other gods are venerated with Him.

In the Genesis passage cited above, God is referring to the physical consummation of male and female. In reality, a marriage license is a societal requirement, or convenience. There is no biblical injunction to obtain a marriage license. This is not to say God does not want it. It is for our own good. It is the symbol of two people saying something to each other and to society about their commitment and their intention.

If a marriage license is not required of God, why do we need one?

Is it really necessary to establish a commitment to one another? The biblical answer is resoundingly yes.

The essence of this argument was given to me from a young engineer I met in a hotel in England. He didn't need a "piece of paper" to allow him to live with his girl friend.

"Do you really believe," I asked, "that a marriage license is not important? Suppose you want to borrow money for a car. You pick out the one you want, then you go to the bank to acquire the money. You tell the banker you are willing to make periodic payments on it for the specified time, and then you say to the banker, 'Now since I don't think the loan papers are important, you don't need to worry about them. You just give me the money, and I'll go buy the car. In due time, I may get around to going to the trouble to obtain a title, but I want to see if I really like the car first.' Will he give you money for the car?"

I continued, "Let me give you another example of why your logic is faulty. Suppose I was able financially, and I desired to buy a new house from you next summer. One of the reasons I want your house is because of what it contains, and I know having it will open up a whole new world of opportunities, enjoyments, and pleasures. I will sign the papers for ownership next summer. But, I tell you, 'Since I will be buying the house next summer anyway, I want to take it over now. It will be all mine eventually anyway.' Would you agree to that? Of course not! Yet, when a young couple says, 'Well, since we are in love, and will eventually get married anyway, let's go all the way now,' it is the same foolish thinking that would not work under any other similar situation."

A young couple needs a marriage license, and a marriage ceremony in a church, in front of family and friends. After an appropriate period of courtship, their two lives will have a chance to slowly blend together emotionally and psychologically without the encumbrances of secret sex muddying the waters.

What is the message God intended our bodies to convey?

God had a purpose in making our bodies the way they are beyond what was necessary to reproduce ourselves. He could have made it necessary for woman to lay eggs and then sit on them for nine months to make them hatch. Why didn't He do it that way?

One reason is God wanted a bonding between mother and child to develop. But He also wanted to emphasize our need as male and female, as husband and wife for one another. Think about this for a moment: He made our bodies to say, "I find completeness in my spouse."

In this unity God balanced the halves to make them work. He made men physically stronger, generally bolder, and more often logic-focused. He made women generally weaker physically, but generally stronger emotionally, supportively and creatively. To balance out the physical weakness, He gave her a built-in radar system!

How do we suffer if we abridge this moral law of God?

Proverbs makes it quite clear, "He who commits adultery has no sense; he who does it destroys himself" (6:32 RSV).

Seven Ways We Harm Ourselves

Future contentment is damaged.

The young engineer from England that I wrote about earlier also told me he couldn't get married because of the way the tax laws were structured in England. They each got a greater tax deduction by being single than if they were married. I responded, "But to save money aren't you giving up something more precious?" "What, for example?" "Well, since you were not committed enough to bother with getting married, and since she was not committed enough to bother with a ceremony, suppose you get terminally ill. Will she be committed enough to stay with you?" "Well I think so." "Are you sure? That's not the emphasis you are putting on your relationship."

But then he told me too, that his girlfriend had had a son from another "arrangement," and that he had had a child with another live-in lover, so he could not afford to get married. I responded, "Can't you see that your previous 'arrangement' is part of the reason you cannot live normally now? What you and your girl friend did out of your own choice back then is inevitably severely restricting you from having full contentment today. And what you are doing now is pulling in the limits of your maneuverability to find fulfillment in the future. You are cutting the throat of your own future contentment."

It puts the wrong emphasis on relationships.

Basing relationships on sex before marriage masks over delicate differences that will cause problems later in marriage. Sex must be kept in strict control before marriage so that a man and a woman can get to know one another as people. This assures they are brought together because of merging personality needs rather than satisfying physical lusts.

If a couple gets involved in sex before marriage, their creative powers are directed to the wrong things at the wrong time and in the wrong way. Vital and important differences are kept from surfacing until after marriage, when by then it is too late to deal with them. All the seeds for divorce are in a relationship where a couple practices sex before marriage. Separation because of "incompatibility" becomes most likely.

During my college years, I developed a close relationship three different times with three different young ladies. In each incident the relationship blossomed enough for us to consider marriage. But in each incidence there were those significant personality differences that finally pushed us apart. I have looked back many, many times, always with thanks to God that we were smart enough not to allow sex to interfere with that process.

No one knows just how much premarital sex leads to divorce, but we may have an indication. As more and more teenagers engage in sex before marriage, the higher goes the divorce rate. "Today more than half of all teenagers—boys and girls—have had sex by the age of 18. . . . Fewer than half the teens who give birth out of wedlock marry within the next few years. Those who do marry are twice as likely to divorce in five years as women who marry in their 20s" (*Reader's Digest,* Sept. 1996, pp. 49, 52).

Only a small percentage of the couples who live together before marriage finally find their way to an altar. There is a correlation between premarital sex and divorce. The reason is that the couples merged their bodies too quickly before personality differences got sorted out and before they could determine their emotional needs, strengths, and weaknesses.

Thomson, a Scottish poet of the last century, wrote: "Real glory springs from the silent conquest of ourselves; without that the conqueror is only the first slave."

It destroys one's capacity for commitment.

Marriage depends more on the thermostat of commitment than on the thermometer of love. Love and lust have become so confused in our society that most people cannot tell the difference between them. They spell "love" l-u-s-t and don't recognize the error! Too often, in the presence of lust, love doesn't have a chance to blossom or even to know if it can bloom. Lust keeps suffocating love.

The amount of love possessed by two people is directly related to the container that holds that love. That container is called commitment.

Why did God set our body clocks to go off early? Why did He not make the sexual drives come to life later so we would not all have to struggle so hard to stay chaste? It would have been easier. But in that case the love that would have developed would have been so much more shallow and less binding.

If God had not given us a chance to build for marriage before marriage, the fabric of commitment through containment could not have been woven. This fabric is woven between puberty and the marriage altar. We can only arrive at commitment through a period of abstinence. When each opportunity to violate sexual purity is resisted before marriage, a stronger marriage bond is possible.

It is somewhat like banking. Suppose I would go to a bank and fill out a withdrawal slip requesting $1000. Not finding an account in my name, the teller would then ask if I had an account there. I would reply, "No, but I saw a report in the newspaper yesterday. Your bank has assets of two hundred million dollars. Ma'am, all I want is $1000." She will reply, "Sir, don't you understand how this bank works? You have to make deposits in this bank until you have accumulated $1000, then you can withdraw it. But not until."

The period between puberty and the marriage altar might be viewed as the period of deposits. If the deposits are not made, the assets will not be there when needed. By denying ourselves of sex with others before marriage, we strengthen our resolve for the one and only. We are then able to more firmly seal our marriage vows when they are made.

By refusing the urge to take the fruits of sex before marriage, we expand the container called commitment or, by our acceptance of the temptation, shrink that container. We can only have as much love as the container of commitment will hold. The reason some couples' marriages do not last is because their container, as a result of sexual promiscuity before marriage, has become a thimble in size. Although it is full of love, there is not enough to splash over more than a few years at most in marriage.

There is a sense in which Christianity is a system of self-discipline. There are those who would try to force Christian principles on society. There is no question but that society would be better off if such principles were followed, but they are of little value to the holder of them if he does not regard them from the heart.

Why does God desire that we learn to discipline ourselves? Quite simply because we never really know ourselves until we have denied ourselves. The touchstone of our character is to be found at the altar where we sacrifice our unbridled ambitions, covetous desires, self-centered action, and lusts.

Augustine's words here are apropos: "Would you have your flesh obey your spirit? Then let your spirit obey your God. You must be governed, that you may govern."

Since sex is the strongest motivation we have, there is a link with other components of our personalities.

The one who can't control his sex drives also has difficulty controlling other areas requiring self-discipline. The one who liberally dispenses sex finds greater difficulty being frugal and responsible in many other areas of life.

Take for examples one's spending habits. Being able to select and stick to goals and the ability to make right decisions is an important discipline. Our abilities are influenced by how sex is treated. When sex is not kept in its God-intended place, controlling and mastering self generally gets more difficult. If one cannot master his passions, his passions will master him.

A Scottish poet had this to say about the importance of self-discipline:

> The discipline which corrects the baseness of worldly passions, fortifies the heart with virtuous principles, enlightens the mind with useful knowledge, and furnishes it with enjoyment from within itself, is of more consequence to real felicity, than all the provisions we can make of the goods of fortune.

Sex before marriage weakens the very thing marriage depends on for its growth and continued existence—trust.

A young man may say to a girl, "I love you too much to wait." She is so convinced of his love she yields to his argument. Then after marriage, he goes on a business trip that takes him out of town for a few days. Thoughts begin to invade her mind such as, "He said he could not wait until marriage. Will he now be able to wait until he gets home?" Then his wife develops doubt, distrust, and suspicion, a direct result of sexual activity before marriage.

James MacDonald, an English prime minister in the early part of twentieth century, once wrote: "To be trusted is a greater compliment than to be loved."

If the barriers are broken down before marriage, they very probably will not be there after marriage when they are needed to protect that relationship. It is simple barnyard psychology that when a cow has found a weakness in a fence and gets out, she will continually go back to the same spot again and again. When the pressures, the differences of opinions, the disagreements come after marriage, as they surely will, the temptation is going to be much harder to resist if the fruit has been tasted before marriage.

It can lead to sexual dysfunction and aberrant behavior.

I recall the time in an introductory Bible class when I was talking about how young people who were engaging in sex before marriage were doing something that could come back to haunt them later. It caused a young star football quarterback to come to me. He admitted that he and his girl friend were meeting regularly at some motel every weekend and having sex.

I expressed my concern that they might come to regret what their activity was doing to both of them. "Do you realize," I told him, "that your relationship is of necessity being built on secrecy and you are having to be underhanded about what's going on. You are pretending something is not happening that is happening. You would not be hiding what you are doing otherwise. And you are very probably having to lie about what is going on to keep a modicum of decency. And I am worried what will happen between the two of you when you finally do get married."

He said they couldn't get married because his girl friend's parents didn't approve of their going together and they could not afford it until next summer anyway. They were planning to marry then. My advice to him was to either get married or quit the underhanded sexual encounters. I told him that before God there was a sense that he was really already married.

Dr. Mark Cosgrove, a psychology professor friend of mine, recently told me, "One of the greatest problems in young people engaging in sex before marriage is the high tendency towards impotency it causes after marriage. Many married men are coming for help who can't seem to function as a husband in marriage. For so long they have played with sex in secrecy and stealth, that they cannot handle it in an open and free manner." They are irresistibly drawn to another relationship that has the excitement of another conquest, another stolen passion, another secret spin.

Then sometimes, not finding ability to function in normal ways, people turn to aberrant behavior such as homosexuality, sodomy, bestiality, or even into chains, whips, and straps.

The most telling physical damage is the multiple millions of young people, men and women, suffering from incurable venereal diseases such as AIDS, herpes, genital warts, clymidia, syphilis, and gonorrhea. It is a given fact that if sexual containment before marriage and sexual fidelity in marriage were practiced, in a generation or two all of the sexually transmitted diseases would be far better controlled.

It can lead to emotional division and loss.

Consider also, that whenever sexual union is attained before, after, or outside of marriage, the "one-fleshness" spoken about in Genesis 2:24 brings about a union where two people become emotionally joined. That fusion is so deep that it is impossible to withdraw two wholes from the one that has been merged. There is a sense in which a couple can only withdraw from such a union with two halves. Then another union is tried, but one can only bring one half to that union and from it one can only take away one fourth, then from another, one eighth, then one sixteenth and endless other divisions.

Perhaps the words of Ralph Waldo Emerson are best used to close this chapter. "Every personal consideration that we allow, costs us heavenly state. We shall lose the thrones of angels for a short and turbulent pleasure."

The Eighth Commandment

You shall not steal (Exodus 20:15).

This is a basic commandment and a necessary part of the Christian ethic. It is a necessary part of living together in a family. It is necessary to society, for without it social relationships are strained and it becomes almost impossible to develop friendships.

The Bible places strong emphasis on being honest. Ezekiel the prophet commends "a righteous man who does what is just and right" and "does not commit robbery" (18:5, 7). The prophet continues to describe how this man is honest and generous. But then he tells of this man's son who is a robber and does just about all other "detestable things" that his father knows to be wrong. He concludes, "his blood will be on his own head" (vv. 12-13).

Stealing from Others Is Like Stealing from God

The premise we have been working from is that a violation of any one of the commandments is injurious to the one committing the offense. How is it so in this case? To begin, it is impossible to maintain a good relationship with God if one steals. Property is viewed in the Bible as a gift from God. The LORD owns everything in heaven and earth (Psalm 24:1), and He has entrusted the earth "to the children of men" (Psalm 115:16). God's gift is never pictured as a gift with no strings attached; it is given to help people develop stewardship.

Jesus makes very clear in the parable of the talents (Matthew 25:14-30) that one cannot receive earthly things and not be responsible for how they are used. If one of the men had stolen from another to increase his holdings, there is little doubt but that he would have received a judgement similar to the one who refused to invest even his one talent. The owner probably would have said, "You wicked, lazy servant, instead of investing your talent to make it grow, you stole from me to add to your amount, because stealing from one of my servants is stealing from me!" So, there is a sense in which stealing from another individual is in reality taking from God. They want to take over control of God's ordained distribution system and rearrange it by appropriating what belongs to other people so they can make it their own.

The person who steals shifts the emphasis to himself and the item he wants to possess. The more he focuses on self and on things, the less he has his focus on God.

Stealing Erodes One's Personality and Relationships

When property is elevated above people and relationships, the thing desired becomes more important than it ought. It increasingly becomes the end to which life is directed while people and relationships suffer accordingly. A friendship will be broken when the element of trust has been undermined by a theft or the fear of it. Even though no theft may have occurred, the possibility of it alone is enough to sabotage any meaningful rapport.

A couple who cannot trust each other's respect for private property cannot build a home. Education is thwarted when a student opts to steal answers; a teacher is caused to suspect that it is happening even when it may not be! Business partnerships are doomed to failure and will soon dissolve if the members look at each other suspiciously.

As with nearly every other sin, the thief has to lower his self-respect to be able to steal. He then has to lower his appreciation of others until he perceives them to be no higher than himself. If that person should want something he doesn't have, he convinces himself to take it.

Stealing Impairs One's Initiative and Creativity

While the first commandment is the foundation of all morality, this one is the touchstone of our economic system. This system is built on rewards for hard work, initiative, and creativity. A thief twists his God-given gift of creativity and ability to make a contribution to society. Instead, he focuses on how he can take advantage of getting the reward for another person's initiative and creativity.

A thief also reverses the God-given right to own private property that has come from working, earning, saving, and having. He wants the fruit of another person's labor without having to earn it. God intended that what we own would be the end result of honest work and frugality. Goods that we don't work to obtain are not viewed with the same appreciation or treated in the same way.

A mother I remember once bragged about how her son was so "lucky." He was always finding money someone had lost. She did not realize he was stealing and covering his crimes with lying. Some parents dismiss small thefts of their children instead of confronting them with the sin of stealing. Such parents should not be shocked when their child, grown into a young adult, is accused of grand theft.

There is an old English proverb that says, "Opportunity makes the thief."

Super markets and other stores that have self-checkouts, while saving money by not having clerks serve customers, make stealing much easier and a more undetectable crime.

There is a growing kind of theft that is viewed as the work of a clever person. The person who can take something that is not theirs and get away with it is almost admired. Not long ago a Wall Street insider sold what were called junk bonds. He made billions, not only for himself but for numerous other speculators as well; yet it had all been at the expense of millions of investors. Because insider information was used to make and sell the bonds, they counted on the ignorance of investors to not know what was being done. That is a growing type of stealing.

There have been business acquisitions of other companies where one of the main incentives was to gain access to the accumulated retirement funds of the employees. The new company then raided those funds since they were not required to abide by the contracts of the old company. This is a form of legalized stealing.

There are growing numbers of people who regard income tax evasion as something that is perfectly natural. They do not hesitate to falsify their returns, or to misstate their expenses, or not include all their income. The government is regarded as the thief and one is comfortable with outwitting the state.

People who travel abroad seek to evade the payment of duty on articles they have purchased. They conceal items in their luggage and fail to declare them as they pass through customs.

Another serious and growing problem is employee theft. In the office an employee may use the note paper for his purposes, take the stamp, use the telephone of his employer for private and personal purposes without any kind of compensation. Many employees come to regard themselves underpaid for their work, so they think they have the right to take what they want for their own purposes to make up the deficiency.

All of this is the result of a situation in which strict and scrupulous honesty is out of fashion. Many a person would be shocked at being identified with people who rob banks, burglarize houses, steal from stores, or annex property to which they have no right. We need to understand that a swindle is still a swindle no matter on whom or where it is carried out.

But consider other thefts that do not involve money. Take for example the theft of time. It may well be that this is the greatest theft of all. It is common practice for people to start late and finish early, to extend break periods, or to loaf on the job. Often there is an attempt to "give as little" then "take as much" as possible. All this has brought about shoddy workmanship and has caused the prices of items to rise in accordance with the amount of time that must be charged to manufacture those items.

The Urge to Steal Grows

The desire to steal is insatiable; a successful thief aspires to more attempts and bigger prizes.

An old Persian proverb says, "An egg-thief becomes a camel-thief." When a thief succeeds in the little theft, he is emboldened to try something a little more daring, requiring a bit more adventuresomeness. He is not satisfied with the small and insignificant. His appetite craves a greater challenge until his stealing becomes a game. He does not think of the persons who suffer loss. He sees only himself becoming a key player in the manipulation of time, people, circumstances, and property.

Many people who practice stealing develop a compulsive abnormality called kleptomania. They are driven to take things with little regard to their value or their need of them. One winter evening before dark, I was blowing snow from the driveway of a widow lady living next to me. Across the street three young girls were trying to dislodge their car from a rather large snow bank. I told them to wait a bit until I obtained more gasoline for my blower and then I would take care of the drift that was impeding them. I brought my gas can to the machine, filled the tank, set the can near the street, but in the driveway of the lady's house.

While I was working across the street, I noticed two men in a car stop in the road at the driveway. The driver looked at me and smiled. My first thought was, "Who is he? Should I know him?" Then the car pulled away. It had gone two blocks before I realized that the smiling man's companion had opened his car door and snatched my gas can. The smile was intended only to distract me from being aware of the burglary.

Being the host of a radio call-in talk show, the next morning I started the program with these words: "There are two fellows in this community for whom I have the utmost sympathy. They stole an inexpensive five-gallon gas can that belonged to me. The loss was not great. The container will easily be replaced without depleting my purse. But the sad part is these two did not awaken yesterday morning and decide, 'We need a gas can. Where can we obtain a gas can?' Instead they have been infected with a disease that makes them take whatever they can whether they need it or not. Their initiative and creativity is being misdirected into a conniving chicanery and a scheming conspiracy to escape detection and make off with something they could well have done without."

I have no knowledge if the two men heard me, but I breathed a prayer that if they were listening they would see the wisdom of my remarks. I prayed that they would change the course of their downward slide, and that they would avoid greater thefts and an accompanying loss of personality assets.

Stealing Destroys Relationships

Of necessity a thief has to depersonalize the one from whom he steals. There are some who have difficulty doing that with individuals they know. They prefer to steal randomly from people they don't know. So to them people become things who are not important enough to respect.

Others still have difficulty even depersonalizing people they don't know so as to be able to steal from them. It is a different matter with respect to institutions like the federal government, or to some big corporation for whom they work. It is as if bigness makes a difference.

To some people stealing $10 from a poor person would be considered wrong. But they think being on a job for a rich employer and loafing for half an hour (yet getting paid for it) is considered legitimate. Perhaps the employee thinks he is underpaid, so he takes some company time or assets to make up the difference. A Christian's motto should still be to give a full day's work for a full day's pay.

I once hired a secretary who casually mentioned to me one day that she had loaned her car to her friend who then had a bad accident with it. She said to me, "I am suing my friend." I responded, "Well, that is one good way to lose a friend."

"Oh no," she replied, "we are in this together. When we get the award we plan to split the money between us."

Defrauding an insurance company in such a way may be done legally, and one may get away with it, but that is still stealing no matter from which side it is viewed. I might add that when I informed the president of the company of her plans, the young lady was fired. She lost her job not just because of that incident but also for her incompetence. Her carelessness in her standard of honesty had affected her work ethic as well.

It is wrong to go willfully into debt and depend on filing for bankruptcy rather than repaying the debt. For if one has to go into bankruptcy, creditors will lose money. Such an arrangement is often little short of legalized stealing.

Years ago I worked for a printing company engaged in printing religious literature. As the company struggled, they acquired a manager who was a Christian and a very astute businessman. He began to sign contracts with companies that gave him several thousand dollars for old equipment if he in return would "lease" new equipment with an arrangement whereby after so many years he would own the equipment.

A windfall of money was coming in, but the debt was climbing astronomically. Being his plant manager, I then began to notice his method of operating also involved ordering skids of paper from certain companies. After letting his payables become delinquent until the companies threatened to take action, he would give them an offer. He would be glad to settle with them for 40 cents on the dollar; but if they refused and he had to go into bankruptcy, they would only receive 10 cents on the dollar.

Considering this legalized stealing, I soon left the company. The businessman eventually lost the company and just about everything else he had. Although he had been a wealthy man at one time, he died nearly a pauper.

Understanding must be given for those who, through unexpected emergencies of life or unanticipated turns in fortune, find themselves unable to get back on an acceptable track. Bankruptcy laws are there for legitimate use. Still we must affirm that this eighth commandment is against stealing in all its forms and financial responsibility is expected of all who follow the Lord. It is often better to be on the safe side and do without rather than to pile on excessive debt.

As stated previously, I hosted a radio call-in program for thirteen years called "Action Line." Occasionally I would interview an author of a recently written book. One book entitled, *I Went Bankrupt, And I'm Glad I Did*, fascinated me. The author came with his lawyer. As was my custom, I read the book before I did the interview. I learned that after his bankruptcy, the man had reestablished credit by obtaining a thousand dollars and deposited it in a bank. A few days later he returned and borrowed $900 against the $1000. He took that money to another bank and deposited it. A few days later he returned and borrowed $800 against the last deposit. With the remainder he faithfully made his monthly payments on time.

He told of how he had gone into the inner city of a large metropolitan area and began to purchase houses that had been foreclosed by FHA and remodeled them into rentals. He was now into big money. He had two or three Cadillacs, lived in an expensive home, and vacationed at Acapulco. In the interview, I asked the man if he had paid back his creditors who had lost money on his earlier move into bankruptcy. He told me he had not. At this point I told the man I had a problem with him rolling in money, yet not paying back those to whom he had owed money before. His only response was, "They did not treat me right." He was protected by the law from having to pay them back. Is this not legalized stealing?

Another veiled way of stealing is retaining from our incomes the ten percent tithe that belongs to God. Malachi very candidly calls it "robbing" God. Properly viewed, we earn only what God enables us to earn and acquire only what God permits us to acquire. He is deserving of all the "first fruits" of our labors.

While we may find it necessary to have cars and property that are financed by some financial institution, we need always to keep in mind that God must hold the first mortgage.

I recall the time a young man, recently converted and growing in faith, came to me after one Sunday morning sermon. He succinctly stated his question, "Should I tithe my income?" The question was motivated mainly because his wife had gone into the hospital in the seventh month of her pregnancy and prematurely delivered her baby, who was now in an incubator. While she was there their six-year-old son had fallen off about six steps and seemed to be paralyzed from his waist down. He too was rushed to the hospital.

My young member then told me, "I have no insurance and even if I paid all my salary each week, my debt would be increasing monumentally. Should I tithe my income at this time?"

I responded, "I don't take your question lightly; I understand your dilemma but I must fall back on my understanding of what God's Word teaches. I believe it is well-summarized in this statement, 'If you honor God, God will honor you.'"

Being a young pastor with little experience, I must admit that I had second thoughts about what I had said. Had I counseled a young father into bankruptcy? But I knew I was correct in my understanding of the Word.

I was relieved and blessed the day I looked out our picture window and saw this young man stop, get out of his car and bound across the street to my front door. I invited him in. He had a broad grin on his face. He said, "You will never believe what happened!" "Try me!" I responded. This is the story he told.

"Being a Ford mechanic, I needed some parts to complete an overhaul. I had to go to Indianapolis to get the parts. It was Friday. Driving along, I was passing the large Ford assembly plant when it seemed something said to me, 'Why don't you go in and apply for a job?' My immediate reaction was, 'I don't need a job; I have a good one.' But the voice persisted, 'Go in and apply for a job.' I wheeled my car around, parked, walked into the Personnel Office, and asked if they were hiring. Without a word the man shoved an application form out to me.

"I sat down and filled it out, listing my experience as a Ford mechanic, my years of employment, and my weekly income. When I returned it to the personnel officer, he glanced over it and exclaimed, 'I can't believe this! I just now received notice that our parts department manager has had to leave his job immediately and we need someone with your background for such a position.' After looking down at my salary figure he said, 'We have a job for you starting Monday morning and if you take it, we will double your salary.'" Then the young man added, "You were right when you told me, 'If you honor God, God will honor you.'"

The "windows of blessing" from heaven had been opened and financial blessings were being heaped upon him.

Jesus made very clear that "having" was conditioned on proper "giving." Malachi broadcasts God's promise that He will open the heavens and pour out blessings on the tither that he will not be able to contain. While this may not always involve money, sometimes that is the end result.

Stealing Causes Financial Loss

A contractor in Brooklyn had endured severe financial loss. He was teetering on the brink of insolvency. He began to try to catch his balance by substituting sub-standard material in his projects whenever there was a probability it would not be detected. He took other short cuts he would not have considered doing before his difficulty.

Hearing about his plight, a wealthy brother-in-law came to him offering to give him the contract to build his newly planned beautiful and expensive house. The contract was signed. The blueprint listed all the materials that were to be used; they were all top grade.

The contractor saw in this situation a chance to regain his financial footing. Across the board he ordered inferior material from what had been specified. He cut back on the quality of the cement work; he used every short-cut possible. Anything that could not be detected was done with shoddy haste. He was stealing from his brother-in-law, but he thought the brother-in-law would never know and he would be a long way towards solvency.

In due time the house was completed. The contractor took the keys to his brother-in-law who, upon their reception, promptly returned them to his relative along with a signed deed and said, "I had this house built for you and my sister. It is yours debt free." Needless to say, the contractor was filled with regret. In trying to cheat his relative, he had actually cheated himself.

Though it may not be as easily discernible as with the contractor, when one cheats God by taking from Him what is His, we are in reality taking from our own pocket. By robbing God, we deny ourselves some future benefit.

Stealing Requires Restitution

The law of the Old Testament certainly condemns stealing, but it gives equal attention to the penalty for it. The restitution of the stolen thing with additional penalties paid by the perpetrator is considered as important as the punishment of the criminal. Restitution had to be made. While Old Testament law wanted to see the criminal punished, it was also eager to see the victim compensated.

It is interesting to note that Jewish law considered theft by night as doubly criminal. Exodus 22:2 states that if a robber by night was killed by a householder in defense of his property, no guilt was attached to that householder.

Exodus 22:1-4 states, "If a man steals an ox or a sheep and slaughters it or sells it, he must pay back five head of cattle for the ox and four sheep for the sheep. . . . A thief must certainly make restitution, but if he has nothing, he must be sold to pay for his theft. If the stolen animal is found alive in his possession—whether ox or donkey or sheep—he must pay back double." According to Proverbs 6:30-31, that which is stolen must be restored sevenfold, even "though it costs him all the wealth of his house." Numbers 5:7 informs us that if a thing is taken fraudulently from anyone, it must be repaid in full plus one-fifth of its value.

Ezekiel 33:15 is even stronger, saying that if the wicked wishes man to live, the first thing he must do is to restore that which he has stolen.

During my early days as a junior in high school, I tried out for the lead part in the class play. At casting time I was awarded the part. The director then informed us that practice would be held every Tuesday and Thursday night from seven until nine and on Saturdays from ten to noon.

Since I was from a poor family, I knew that if I wanted to attend college I would have to work and save. A few weeks before the tryouts I had been hired to work from four until midnight at a local tomato-canning factory.

After the casting meeting ended, I went to the director and asked her if she would allow a stand-in to take my place on the weeknights. I told her I would learn the lines and be at practice faithfully each Saturday. She denied my request and said she would have to recast the part. Asking her to delay the move a few days, I connived another plan. I knew the foreman would not allow me to miss six hours each week to practice for the play. I was one of several young men on the packing line who took turns so as to relieve fatigue. Aware that I was not too closely supervised, I got the guys together and agreed to work harder for them until 6:30 on the two week nights in question, if they would cover for me until 9:30 when I would return. If anyone, including the boss, asked where I was, I told them they could say, "Oh, he is taking his break now."

With their cooperation, the plan worked. I parked my bike outside the back door of the plant, made my practice times, and then returned as planned. I was never caught. I forgot all about the whole episode.

A few months later I gave my heart to the Lord. I attended a year of college. The following summer, as I was trimming the hedge of my parent's property, the Lord reminded me of how I had cheated the factory out of six hours of labor each week, had been paid for it, and that I would have to make it right.

I did not know if the superintendent of the plant would order me to pay back the money immediately, which I did not have, or if he would have me arrested. But knowing God would help me, I fearfully made my way to the plant. After meeting the man, I told him who I was and of how I had cheated the factory. I informed him that the reason I had come was because I was now a Christian and was trying to clear my past. I told him I did not know how many hours I had actually been paid when I was not even in the factory, but if he would give me a figure of how much I owed the factory, I would repay it just as soon as possible.

After thinking out loud a bit about not knowing how many hours were involved and how the records were all filed, he said to me, now addressing me by my first name, "Wilbur, I think the best thing is simply to forget it. But let me tell you this. If you ever want a job, I want you to come and see me!"

There was no better way to witness to this man than by simply confessing my sin to him. What I thought was going to be my worst restitution, became one of my most cherished blessings.

CHAPTER XI

The Ninth Commandment

You shall not bear false witness . . .
(Exodus 20:16 NASB).

What would life be like without a tongue? There is such a thing as non-verbal communication, but its "vocabulary" is very limited. Relationships involving trade, education, health, and growth in general require spoken expressions. The tongue is so important a faculty that it demanded the focus of two out of the ten commandments, lest the tongue fly out either against God (commandment three) or against other people (commandment nine).

If we go to a doctor for a diagnosis of an illness, he will ask us to stick out our tongue. He knows that it tells much about the diseases of the body. When the tongue speaks, it reveals if there are diseases of the heart and mind.

We differ from animals in our soul or spirit, which is "created in the image of God." We are also eminently different in the use of the tongue. We are more dangerous and yet have higher promise than all of the other creatures God has made. The tongue is at once our best part and our worst part. It can either speak truth or it can lie.

The writer of Proverbs 3:3 recognized the importance of the source from which the tongue speaks. "Let love and faithfulness never leave you; bind them around your neck [at the base of the tongue], write them on the tablet of your heart [the well spring of the tongue]."

Truth in the heart is the best assurance against the tongue lying or commiting other gross sins. David realized when he committed his most heinous sin that it came from his heart—a heart where truth had not found permanent lodging. He said in his confession to God, "Surely you desire truth in the inner parts; you teach me wisdom in the inmost place" (Psalm 51:6).

In the early years of the return of the Jews from the Exile, the prophet Zechariah was trying to help the people of Jerusalem to see what the future held for them. He affirmed that the LORD said, "Jerusalem will be called The City of Truth" (8:3). Later in the same passage, he admonishes the people, "These are the things you should do: Speak the truth to each other . . . do not love to swear falsely . . . " (vv. 16-17).

Paul no doubt had this passage in mind when he admonished, "Therefore, each of you must put off falsehood and speak truthfully to his neighbor, for we are all members of one body" (Ephesians 4:25 NASB).

The apostle, however, was going back beyond the expression to the thoughts that breed the expression, when he wrote, "Whatever is true, whatever is noble, whatever is right, whatever is pure, whatever is lovely, whatever is admirable . . . think about such things" (Philippians 4:8).

In *The Professor at the Breakfast Table,* Oliver Wendell Holmes wrote, "Truth is tough. It will not break, like a bubble, at a touch; nay, you may kick it about all day like a football, and it will be round and full at evening."

Why is not bearing false witness so critical to our contentment? Let us look at four reasons.

To Preserve Justice

In an essay on "Prudence," Ralph Waldo Emerson says, "Every violation of truth is not only a sort of suicide in the liar, but it is a stab at the health of human society."

The ninth commandment is a call for the sanctity of truth in all areas of life. During the years of wandering in the desert, the time when the commandments were given, Israel had what is best described as a desert society. In that kind of situation, a crime committed was so magnified that it would reach beyond the intended victim. A conviction on the basis of false witness would be equivalent to murder.

While God would have had that situation in mind, He was giving laws that were applicable in every society for all time and in any place.

One who bears false witness against another could ultimately lead to a complete travesty of justice and destroy the effectiveness of a court. Any society depends heavily on the truthfulness of the members who make up its parts. Justice cannot be rendered when truth is disregarded.

The prosecution of crimes depends heavily upon witnesses who saw or heard what happened. If what a witness says he heard or saw is not based in truthfulness, justice cannot be rendered.

In biblical times, much weight was generally put on always speaking the truth. But the Bible is not the only place where one finds a recognition of the damage falsehood engenders. In the famous Hammurabi's Code, the law read, "If a man accused another man in a charge of murder against him, but has not proved it, his accuser shall be put to death." A judge could render a hundred just verdicts, but when one unjust judgment is made on the basis of a false witness, the judge's creditability as well as justice is damaged.

God's concern was for Israel to safeguard against falsehood having a part in the conviction of a person. Deuteronomy 17:7 makes it clear that the two or more who witnessed a crime were to throw the first stone. They would be guilty of murder if they were lying. This helps us understand Jesus' reply to the Pharisees who wanted a woman stoned who had been taken in adultery (John 8:7). They had brought her to Jesus, knowing of His forgiving nature. They hoped He would disregard the Law of Moses, so they could find cause to accuse Him. At first He bowed down and wrote in the sand. They closed in as though they finally had Jesus in a corner. Their questions persisted. He raised himself and said, "He who is without sin among you, let him be the first to throw a stone at her." Then He bowed down to write again. Was Jesus writing in the sand the sins of which the accusers were guilty? Or was He giving time for the thoughts of the guilty to accuse them?

While either may have been the case, there is also the possibility that Jesus was taking the Mosaic Law further. He may have been requiring the one who threw the first stone not only to know positively the woman was guilty, but also to have no unforgiven sin.

There seems to be no doubt that the woman was guilty. She was "caught in the act." But it is likely those who had not witnessed the sin were trying to testify to its fact when they had no firsthand knowledge of what happened. The only one who could give firsthand testimony would also be condemning himself, since he'd joined her in adultery. Those who came before Jesus were therefore "false witnesses," and the Lord was making them a party to the condemnation. Jesus was making it clear that one who was guilty of a certain sin had no right whatsoever condemning another person guilty of a sin.

False witnesses alone caused the death of Naboth, the man who owned a vineyard desired by Ahab (1 Kings 21). Because he would not sell it to King Ahab nor accept another piece of better ground in trade, Ahab returned to his palace "sullen and angry" (v. 4).

Finding Ahab on his bed refusing to eat, Jezebel asked what it was that caused such demeanor. When she learned the cause she asked him, "Is this how you act as king over Israel?" Then with a calculated precision she told him to "Get up and eat! Cheer up. I'll get you the vineyard of Naboth" (v. 7).

Jezebel sent letters to the elders and nobles in Ahab's name, telling them to proclaim a fast. She wanted the guise of religion to underscore the seriousness of the victimization. Then she had Naboth set at the head of the people. Next she gave instruction for them to find two worthless men who would willingly lie under oath that they had witnessed Naboth cursing God and the king. She then sealed those letters with the seal of the king.

In a society where extreme poverty exposed men to such bribery, the town officials had no difficulty in purchasing the false testimony. With monstrous lies Naboth was murdered.

Leviticus 19:16 was inspired to avoid such happenings: "Do not do anything that endangers your neighbor's life." It was impossible for justice to be served because of Jezebel's evil intent and the purposeful lies of the two perjurers.

Charles Caleb Colton was a nineteenth-century English writer and clergyman. He once observed, "Pure truth, like pure gold, has been found unfit for circulation, because men have discovered that it is far more convenient to adulterate the truth than to refine themselves."

To Maintain Credibility

Not only is a judge's credibility damaged when he renders a judgment based on a false witness, but when a person is known once to have lied, whatever he says afterwards sounds false however true it may be. Stealing is bad because it robs one of his property; false witness is bad because it robs one of his good reputation.

The words of the wise writer of Proverbs are: "The tongue of the wise commends knowledge, but the mouth of the fool gushes folly. . . . The tongue that brings healing is a tree of life, but a deceitful tongue crushes the spirit" (Proverbs 15:2, 5).

How unfortunate it is to society that lying has become an acceptable form of communication. In schools, lying for grades is a common practice. In one recent survey it was determined that two-thirds of the students admitted cheating recently on an exam. Lying for promotion is frequently done in our day. Two out of five people said they would lie if necessary to keep their job.

People who have lower self-esteem often lie. They want to appear better than they are. They want others to think more highly of them, so they say what will give them a better image even though it is not factual.

In a recent study of the journal entries of 77 students at the University of Virginia, no less than 1500 lies were recorded. It was determined that one in every three times these students "fibbed" was to enhance the liar's image.

At this juncture we should note that we can best enhance self-image by avoiding sin. When a person commits a wrongful deed, it is rather common for the perpetrator to say to himself, "Why did I do that? I knew better!" Then comes the resultant drop in self-image. The lower one perceives himself to be, the more he allows sins to be committed. And soon he loses control. J. C. Macaulay considered a lie "a refuge of weakness. A man of courage is not afraid of the truth."

Of course, the object of God's grace is to restore by salvation the self-image that was lost through sin. Then the work of the Holy Spirit is available to help one regain self-mastery by making the control center of the heart cooperative and supportive in refraining from image-damaging sin.

In the study of college students at the University of Virginia mentioned earlier, many lied to spare the listener's feelings or to help them avoid embarrassment.

While the desire to help people better cope with life may be a worthy motive, to exercise it at the expense of the truth is wrong no matter how accepted a practice it has become.

Sometimes the truth hurts, but that does not justify substituting it with a lie. Once a person discovers he has been told a lie, there is a rupture in open and free communication. From then on, there is added uncertainty about the veracity of what the speaker says. Additionally, the person who was lied to may well opt for a choice based on the untruth told. In a sense the liar has coerced that choice.

It is noteworthy that in Mark's account of Jesus telling the rich young ruler what he had to do to inherit eternal life (10:17-19), after citing the ninth commandment, Jesus added, "Do not defraud." In itself this is not a commandment, but defrauding is an end result of lying when it causes a person to make a decision that would not have been made had it not been for the lie.

It may not always be wise to tell the whole truth in a given moment, especially when the truth is not spoken in love. Without the wisdom of what is best left unsaid, such action can alienate people and destroy their friendship. To always tell the truth does not make it necessary for one to become rude and tactless. Paul admonished the Ephesians to speak "the truth in love" (4:15).

A doctor who has just detected cancer in a patient does not have to deny it if asked. Depending on the person, however, there might be a more appropriate time later to reveal his findings.

An eighteenth-century medical doctor by the name of Thomas Fuller once said, "All truth is not to be told at all times." Perhaps a doctor knows more readily the truth of such a statement. Sometimes if a truth hurts or cuts, it is best not spoken, but a lie should never be thought an acceptable alternative.

We have all heard someone say, "It is the truth, so let it be said" or, "If the truth hurts, let it hurt." The wiser course of action is found in Proverbs 12:18 (NASB): "There is one who speaks rashly like the thrusts of the sword, but the tongue of the wise brings healing."

Francis Quarles, a seventeenth-century English author, observed, "Give not your tongue too great liberty, lest it take you prisoner. A word unspoken is, like the sword in the scabbard, yours. If vented, your sword is in another's hand. If you desire to be held wise, be so wise as to hold your tongue. . . . A fool's heart is in his tongue; but a wise man's tongue is in his heart."

To lie is to trade a truth for an untruth—a bad trade. To speak a truth that is unkind, even unloving, is to use truth as a weapon to cut and maim. Just because something is the truth is no cause to always speak it. A person is cheated not to have sense enough to speak well and wisdom enough to speak wisely.

Perhaps a distinction should be made between partial truth and an untruth. After Saul had sinned away the opportunity for his family to rule the throne of Israel, Samuel is told to go to Bethlehem to anoint the next king. Samuel protested, "How can I go? Saul will hear about it and kill me." The LORD told him "Take a heifer with you and say, 'I have come to sacrifice to the LORD'" (1 Samuel 16:2). Samuel knew he had no right to speak an untruth, but Saul had forfeited his right to know all the truth. So God permitted him to tell just part of the whole truth.

George Herbert was an eighteenth-century clergyman and also a metaphysical poet. He wrote in verse:

> Dare to be true: nothing can need a lie;
> A fault which needs it most, grows two thereby.

But the ninth commandment is broader than false witness when the life of a person is at stake. This commandment also covers what might be termed tattling and tale-bearing, or repeating untrue or even unkind gossip that could damage a neighbor. The actual Hebrew word here is not "falsehood," but "frivolous, vain words."

Lying is always wrong, whether it is the midwives' lie (Exodus 1:15-19) or anyone else's lie. Scripture repeatedly warns against all falsehoods and commends truth-telling. Proverbs 6:19 (NKJV) goes so far as to say God hates "A false witness who speaks lies, And one who sows discord among brethren."

But the Bible also calls a refusal to come forward as a witness to something that has been seen or learned a "sin" (Leviticus 5:1). The implication is that remaining silent in such a situation is tantamount to lying.

To Maintain Harmony of Personality

In the Bible, lying almost exclusively refers to lying with words. In today's world, one of the most frequent types of lying is done within a person's life. These people are commonly called hypocrites. Those whose lives do not measure up to what they profess do most damage to the cause of

Christ in the Church. Their words say one thing; their lives say another. They cause greater harm because, to the people of the world, they prove the world's ideas about Christianity's inconsistencies and provide an excuse for people to continue in their own sin. Such a hypocrite will cause a young Christian's confidence to weaken. I speak from experience.

I had just graduated from college, had married, and was beginning graduate school. Needing part-time employment, I found it at a local lumberyard. Fortunately, I thought, the manager was the vice chairman of the local board of the church where my wife and I were attending. He had helped me get the job. He actively participated in the services and all aspects of church life. I had great confidence in his faith.

My assignment on this particular morning was to clean the dust off the paint cans shelved in the L-shaped display room. I was at work around the corner and away from the main service counter. I began to overhear a conversation that was amply peppered with swear words. To my amazement many of them sounded as though they were coming from the mouth of the manager. I crept closer to the main counter to make sure. I was right!

I was so shaken with the knowledge, I immediately walked out of the front door of the business, went straight home, and entered the front door of my house weeping. My wife asked what was the matter. I replied, "My faith has just been shaken to its foundation because I just heard the man I believed to be one of the best Christians swearing."

Had my faith been entirely in people instead of in God, the revelation of this man's duplicity might well have caused me to abandon my faith completely. My faith held firm, but it was severely shaken.

Unquestionably, this man did more injury to himself than to me. He could not possess a harmonious personality. In reality he was having to be two different people at different times. If a Christian would appear, he would have to assume one personality; if an old chum came by, he would put on another. But this time another Christian had heard who he really was by what he said, since he did not have the time to "shift gears."

The early-nineteenth-century poet Percy Shelly considered falsehood "a scorpion that will sting itself to death." In the case of the lumberyard manager, he nearly stung another young Christian to death as well.

We were made to possess a personality that results from all of our "notes" being blended and harmonized together in genuineness. A lie may come from one who possesses the truth. But when truth possesses a person, a lie will suffocate, for it can find no breath. God wanted truth to be so much a part of our being that He inspired the writer of Proverbs to say, "Buy the truth and do not sell it." And the very next line says, "Get wisdom, discipline and understanding" (23:23). The implication is that if truth is not purchased, one forfeits also the priceless instructional qualities of wisdom and understanding.

In Plato's *Phaedo* (4th–3rd century B.C.), Socrates noted, "False words are not only evil in themselves, but they infect the soul with evil."

To Maintain Respect for God

God's very being and nature was and is truth. To substitute a lie for the truth is like embracing a false god for that moment.

I quoted earlier the command found in Leviticus 19:16-17. "Do not go about spreading slander among your people. Do not do anything that endangers your neighbor's life." Then follows the phrase, "I am the LORD." This last phrase frequently closes requirements given by God. Such a statement is made when a law of conduct is expressed to show that to disobey it is in reality an affront against God himself.

It is not possible to maintain a proper relationship with God unless one is married to truth. Can one be a loyal husband to truth if he even once cohabits with a lie? Is it even thinkable that a child of both truth and untruth could be unsullied and pure?

Jesus said, "You shall know the truth, and the truth shall make you free" (John 8:32 NASB). The implication can be easily seen; untruths will enslave us.

The Tenth Commandment

You shall not covet . . . (Exodus 20:17).

The first commandment we studied in chapter three had to do with what one thinks. We called the worship of any god other than the LORD *internal idolatry* because it is a sin that occurs in the mind.

Now we learn the last one of the Ten Commandments ends where it all began—with thoughts that harbor the sin of *internal greed*.

Robert South has observed that "Covetousness is both the beginning and the end of the devil's alphabet—the first vice in corrupt nature that moves, and the last which dies."

Jesus was teaching in the middle of His earthly ministry. He had made some pointed remarks directly to the Pharisees. They sensed their authority slipping with the people who had been drinking in the Savior's teaching. On one occasion "a crowd of many thousands had gathered, so that they were trampling on one another" to get closer to Him (Luke 12:1). The scribes and Pharisees had been vehemently cross-examining Him with loaded questions, "waiting to catch him in something he might say" (Luke 11:54).

Sensing the Lord's authority in speaking to the Pharisees, a man stepped from the crowd and requested, "Teacher, tell my brother to divide the inheritance with me" (Luke 12:13). Perhaps he made the request because in Old Testament times, when the law of primogeniture was observed, the eldest son got twice as much inheritance as the other sons, no matter how many there were. If this was the case, the man may have felt the law to be unjust, and he wanted Jesus to amend it for him. The Lord looked deeper than the man's opinion of the law. He recognized the seedbed of the heart from which the request came.

With a tone of rebuke, Jesus replied, "Man, who made Me a judge or an arbiter between you?" Then, with the precision of a surgeon, the Lord cut to the heart of the man's problem: "Watch out! Be on your guard against all kinds of greed; a man's life does not consist in the abundance of his possessions" (Luke 12:14-15).

Note that Jesus used the form of law that in chapter two we called "apodictic." He uses the second person singular as He addressed the man but did not state a punishment. Why? As much with this commandment as with any of the previous nine, the one who covets hurts himself by his own covetousness. Paul succinctly puts it to Timothy this way, "Some people, eager for money, have wandered from the faith and pierced themselves with many griefs" (1 Timothy 6:10).

Covetousness especially causes self-inflicted wounds. Let us look at some of them.

It Leads to Other Sins

Nothing similar to this tenth commandment has ever been found in any of the recently discovered ancient law codes. In our day one would never see such a law on any law books in a courthouse. It simply could not be enforced. It is the one sin that can easily be hidden from the eye. It is generally held today that a person can think what he wants to think as long as he does not injure another person.

We might then consider this sin less important and wonder why God would bother to make it one of the ten. The answer is clear. God certainly does not want people to sin, but more importantly, He does not want them even to consider doing so. If the egg of desire is not even allowed to develop, it cannot hatch. If prevention is emphasized, no infection happens and no cure is needed.

God is also more concerned with the individual and what is happening on the inside. He knows that outward conformity can mask a grasping heart. A person, who has not yet overtly commited another sin as a result of coveting can easily and conveniently disguise his greed.

Leonard Wright calls covetousness "the root of all evil, the ground of all vice."

If this is true, then it is no wonder the Lord considered it important enough to make covetousness conclude the Ten Commandments. It probably would not be too difficult to see this sin included somewhere in each of the first nine.

Even though a person never hears anyone confess to having had the sin of covetousness, perhaps because it may be considered a minor slip, it is certainly not a slap-of-the-wrist infraction. It is deadly because it opens a window and looks longingly at the grossest of other sins. It opens wide the door and invites the sins to move in.

It Turns a Person Inward

Covetousness feeds on satisfying self at the expense of all else. It leads the person who harbors it to come to believe the world was created for him. All it has to offer is his if he wants it, and what he takes he can keep.

Because coveting makes a person continually look inward, he moves like one who looks in a mirror as he backs into the future. Who he is gets lost as he keeps reaching for what he thinks he needs. Because self is diminished by coveteousness' insatiable appetite, its desires become a hell it doesn't want but can't live without.

The one who covets what someone else has is admitting to a conscious inferiority. Soon he compares himself with other people. He is pleased only with those who are beneath him. He casts a covetous eye on anyone who appears to be more virtuous. Feeling the need to rise above them, he focuses his attention on them, then tries to "stand above" them by pulling them down. In doing so, his "self" gets a euphoric, though false, feeling of virtue.

Benjamin Franklin also noted, "Whoever feels pain in hearing a good character of his neighbor, will feel a pleasure in the reverse. And those who despair to rise in distinction by their virtues are happy if others can be depressed to a level with themselves."

Francis Bacon, the seventeenth-century English author, journalist, scientist, and philosopher, once observed the following: "A man that has no virtue in himself ever envies virtue in others; for men's minds will either feed on their own good, or upon others' evil; and he who wants the one will prey upon the other; and the one who is out of hope to attain to another's virtue will seek to come at [it from every] hand by depressing another's fortune."

It Makes One a Hypocrite

Generally speaking, covetousness operates best in secrecy. One who covets what his neighbor has does not want his neighbor, or anyone else for that matter, to know it. So it becomes necessary to put on a face, an attitude, or a demeanor that hides what he truly thinks and feels inside. He pretends that what is true is not really. He now turns dark inside and increasingly walks on the "shady" side of the street.

The one who covets has to pretend he likes his neighbor, so he will be better apprised of what his neighbor is doing. It makes the coveter lose his genuineness. He has to become a good actor to hide his true feelings. The more he tries to hide, the more he has to hide. His "false face" increasingly becomes an easy mask to hide more thoughts that ultimately develop into misdeeds.

It Destroys Wholesome Relationships

C. S. Lewis, in his book *God in the Dock,* speaks about a relationship which "becomes in the end greedy, naggingly solicitous, jealous, exacting, timorous. It suffers agony when its object is absent—but is not repaid by any long enjoyment when the object is present."

Covetousness makes one egocentric. It destroys one's appreciation of the uniqueness of another. The whole focus of life turns selfish. It makes one want, not because of need but because of greed. It leads to divorce when the opposite sex is involved.

God would have us always consider a person more important than what he may possess at any given time. A coveter, however, depersonalizes an individual, and gives the individual's possessions a higher priority. He reverses the God-ordained order.

He begins to see the person who owns the coveted thing a barrier to having what is coveted. He finds himself disrespecting him. He develops hatred and jealousy, then soon begins to believe his neighbor's rights are impinging on his own.

It Can Make One a Thief

If any one sin is more closely allied to covetousness than any other, it has to be that of stealing. There is a sense in which covetousness and theft are identical twins; they are dressed alike and are nearly always seen together.

D. L. Moody called the one who covets "a thief in a shell." If he covets, he needs only the opportunity to take the object of his inordinate desire, especially if he thinks no one will know, and then he becomes a thief *out of* a shell.

A covetous person may not possess wealth, but wealth possesses him. Some covet because they don't have what they covet. Others have, yet cannot keep from coveting more. They want riches not to enjoy but simply to have. We have all heard of people who have starved themselves in the midst of plenty so they could have more. In effect they cheat and rob themselves from enjoying what is theirs so they will still "have it."

Paul informed Timothy that "people who want to get rich fall into temptation and a trap and into many foolish and harmful desires that plunge men into ruin and destruction. For the love of money is a root of all kinds of evil" (1 Timothy 6:9-10).

It Makes Normal Desires Go Bad

Let's look at some examples from Scripture.

Abraham

God promised Abraham that he would have a "very great reward" (Genesis 15:1). This father of the chosen race-to-be let God know that without a son there could be no reward. Then he informed God that his plan was to "adopt" his servant Eliezer (15:2-3). We know this was often done when couples were childless.

Abraham and Sarah lived in a day when people, especially women, thought life with their mates should always result in children. Not to have any was unacceptable. It was the normal reaction to assume that a barren wife was responsible if there were no children. Societal laws required that she should solve her problem by "setting up" an alternative situation. She suggested to her husband that he accept into their circle a "lesser wife," who was usually a servant girl.

Such a practice in no way pleased the Lord, but the pagan influences were so strong and so embedded that this patriarchal couple resorted to it.

For them to have a child was God's will. He told Abraham clearly that he would have "a son coming from your own body" (Genesis 15:4). As Abraham and Sarah learned, God did not intend it to happen by means of the servant, Hagar.

It was normal for them to covet an offspring, but God wanted it done His way, by means of Sarah. For the moment, though, they failed to trust the LORD. It appears that they thought God had not fulfilled His promise. "Perhaps," they likely reasoned, "He was expecting them to do it their way." So they took the socially approved route. Instead of continuing to trust God not only to do what He had promised, but also to do it His way, they let a normal desire lead them astray.

Moses

While Moses had been raised as the son of Pharaoh's daughter, he had to have learned that his early nurse was indeed his real mother (Exodus 2:7-8). As he grew older it was normal for him to feel a commonality with his people and to despise what the Egyptians were doing to them.

One day he witnessed an Egyptian beating a defenseless Hebrew slave, one of his own. If he was destined to become the great deliverer, he had to have a hatred for what was happening to them. His wanting, even coveting, a liberation for his people was commendable. It was right. It was of God.

But Moses was not content to wait for God's timing. Knowing himself stronger than this particular Egyptian, Moses took matters into his own hands. Thinking no one would see, he killed the overbearing slave driver and buried his body under the sand (Exodus 2:12). His impetuous action cost him his position, his power, and his authority. He lost all he had gained.

Achan

Jericho was to be destroyed. Everything in it was to be "devoted to the LORD" (Joshua 6:17), which meant nothing was to be appropriated as booty. As noted in chapter two of this book, the directive God gave was likely to spare the Israelites sexually transmittable infection from each other or beasts.

"All the silver and gold and the articles of bronze and iron . . . [were] sacred to the LORD and must go into his treasury" (Joshua 6:19).

Jericho was miraculously destroyed, but in the mop-up operation, Achan's covetousness got the best of him. He may have thought the dictum was unnecessary and that things of value, such as a beautiful Babylonian garment, did not have to be destroyed. Nor was it necessary to give all the precious metal to the LORD. He could make better use of some of it.

So by his own words, he "coveted them" (Joshua 7:21). His greed could have caused a plague to break out among the people. And he also stooped so low as to steal from the LORD.

Amnon

It was a short time after David had sinned with Bathsheba that his eldest son began to let his normal sexual drives be directed towards his half-sister, Tamar. In the words of the writer, he "fell in love with Tamar" (2 Samuel 13:1).

To be more candid, Amnon did not have an understanding of love; he was consumed with the covetousness of lust. Tamar was a virgin (2 Samuel 13:2), making it almost impossible for him to get to her. In that day, virginity was a matter of pride. Those who had it were allowed to wear a special robe (2 Samuel 13:18).

Since his desire for what he could not otherwise have sprang from covetousness, he forced himself on her when she would not cooperate with him. His self-centered act destroyed her self-image and ultimately cost Amnon his life.

It Makes Things a God

The human person was built to need a higher level of leadership than one's self. In the hierarchy of His creation, God made animals to serve people in various ways and they are not fulfilled if they cannot do it. For example, a dog needs a master. Without one he reverts to the wild and loses his desire to serve. He becomes self-centered out of a desire to simply exist.

The element within us that needs God gets turned downward toward things. Whatever makes the person feel better, look successful, and appear to be more astute at everything must be acquired. It is of little concern that it may destroy friendships. Though it may make one cagey, he thinks it is a risk worth taking. Increasingly, caution is thrown to the wind. The coveter must have the "thing" to establish a greater credibility. The possibility that the very credibility he covets will be lost by his coveting seems not to occur to him. He becomes increasingly greedy for more.

Normal Desires

There is definitely a good side to coveting. It is when one covets the right things for the right reasons, when one reaches out, not just to have more, but to obtain so as to serve more adequately. Paul identifies it in 1 Corinthians 12:31, when he tells us to "covet earnestly the best gifts." We should intensely desire to please God in all that we do. We should fervently follow the instructions in His Word. We should passionately want to grow in faith. We should ardently love the work of the Lord. This is all a type of wholesome covetousness that should be normal for a growing and maturing child of God.

Indeed, it is a normal desire for a person to express himself. God has given every one of us various types of innate abilities that make us want to give ourselves with diligence to causes of worthy merit. We have energies that are intended to be given sacrificially. We have a certain force of personality that seeks to express itself through caring, helping, and loving.

It is a natural human desire to long for things, to wish to have, and to own. And it is normal for us to take the steps necessary to obtain what is desired. But this natural human tendency must be directed to the right ends. It is not right to "covet" a newer car or a nicer house simply because a neighbor has a nicer one or because people will have a higher regard for us. It is right to want a newer car or better house to more adequately serve the Lord in our work and witness and worship.

It is not good to "covet" status and popularity and position so as to say to people, "Look at me! Look how successful I am! Look how much money I'm making." But it is pleasing to the Lord for one to work hard to achieve a more responsible position, to desire to be elevated because of faithfulness, dependability, loyalty, and honesty. What self-centered coveting fails to obtain, selfless giving often seems to acquire.

These various drives we have are wholesome and healthy only as long as they are blended and balanced by God. This is really not possible for one who has not permitted his heart to be purged of sin. When sin is allowed to remain in a heart, whatever comes from it is lopsided. It is skewed and off center. It is pulled towards the wrong, and it has great difficulty avoiding it. Instead of wanting in order to serve more, it is motivated more often by wanting in order to have more.

Sometimes the wrong emphasis is given to right things. Too little or too much attention is given. It lacks a proper distribution.

It may be that as much or more than any of the other nine commandments, the tenth commandment belies a heart that has not been cured of its carnal twist, its bent towards sinning. Evil thoughts and wrong desires can be hidden from others' view. God's eye alone penetrates inside all the closets of the heart. Unless the converted person has experienced the cleansing that takes away the magnetic pull towards evil, he struggles to keep from coveting.

The three following diagrams should help to better explain the differences. The circles represent three hearts.

The heart of the sinner

The first circle represents the heart of a sinner in which God has no important part. The sections are labeled with the three main things that most people consider important. The item termed "material values" represents not only money but also anything of value that money buys. The person may believe in God. He may even go to church. But while God may occasionally be in his thinking, He is not even permitted a minority opinion. At best He is peripheral. Notice that the three sections look balanced, but in a person's heart they rarely are. The carnal self will make one or another have the dominant emphasis and give it the most attention. It is usually the one that the particular self enjoys most. The other items are pushed into the background.

This person lives life on what might be called the "cafeteria plan"—self-service only. Self must be maximized and gratified. Everything must lead to and blend with that.

The heart of the converted

This second circle represents the heart of one who has accepted Jesus as his Savior. God now has a prominent place in the heart but not a central controlling place. He is important but not all-important. He is given emphasis but no greater and no less than any other emphasis. The person with this kind of heart has learned to compartmentalize his life. When money is needed, money gets the attention. When status is required, status gets the emphasis. And when God needs to be given attention, especially on days like Sunday, He gets the attention.

The heart of the sanctified

In this third diagram, the heart of the sanctified, God is not only present but has the central place. He pervades all. He flavors and colors all. He is the ultimate authority. Self does not seek to express itself for itself. It seeks to express itself for Him. Much effort is given to please Him. The things one possesses become tools to aid in His service. Things of value are sought to better serve His cause. Whatever glory is gained is used to defer to His glory. There is a place for the other items of importance, but they never vie with God for the main emphasis. He is all and in all, the cause for all and the purpose of all. In short, life revolves around Him. There is no better way to live life than to live it without the inner pull of sin. The heart needs to be cleansed of it all.

CHAPTER

Conclusion

Economic and Moral Logic

It was mentioned in chapter eleven that in today's culture and on certain occasions, lying is acceptable. If the end result is thought to be needed and if one needs to improve his view of himself or to spare another person emotional hurt, then lying is in order. This sometimes makes it more difficult to be truthful, especially when it is not popular to do so.

Society's view in general makes it harder for a Christian to pursue a lifestyle that blends easily with all ten of the commandments. It is hoped that this study has helped to underscore the necessity of obeying the commandments if we hope to preserve and expand our happiness.

There is another aspect of society today that causes pressure on Christian conduct that is not generally recognized. It has to do with the relationship of economic logic with moral logic.

Compare for a moment my father's day to our day. For him, economic logic and moral logic were most often parallel. They both had similar ends. Moral logic was, "Don't do something today that will be regretted tomorrow." And economic logic was similar, "Don't encumber yourself financially so as to cheat yourself from economic independence in your old age." My father was especially concerned about avoiding financial poverty after he retired.

So it was a normal practice for him to refrain from contracting too large a debt, or any at all if he could avoid it. He did not want to have to "beg" when he retired. He wanted financial independence in his old age. He wanted his house and car paid for. Therefore, as a family we always had an older car and did not live in quite as nice a house as we might have had. As it happened, Dad did not have to pay so much of his income on interest. He sought to manage debt economically as he sought to manage his life spiritually. Each of these two areas then had similar goals and being thus related, both were easier to do.

Few today espouse the similar economic logic, "Make a few sacrifices today so you will be able to have more tomorrow." Financial institutions, for example, are saying in numerous ways, "Spend tomorrow's assets today. Why wait? You can have it all now." The present generation has little concern about how much interest they have to pay on a desired loan, or the length of time involved before the loan has to be repaid.

All they want to know is the total amount of the monthly payment, not the interest rate nor how long the loan will last! Just how much will it cost them per month? Though such a debt does give them *a bit more* in the short run, it is gained at the loss of *a lot more* in the long run.

So today economic logic is in contrast to the traditional moral logic. Very often, as a direct result of current economic logic, many churches are suffering financially. Why? Because many of the members are encumbering themselves with debt in such large amounts that members cannot find enough money to offer their tithe to the church.

This is not to condemn all debt, for most people would not be able to buy a house at all without some debt. But debt must be contracted wisley for the right things, and in a balanced and affordable amount, so as not to be denied more in the future.

I was recently told about a young plumber who, though good at his profession, could not always find enough work to pay all the bills, one of which was his house payment. So during lean months, when he did not have enough money to make ends meet, he simply used his MasterCard to make the mortgage payment. This continued for several years and the credit card company conveniently raised his charge limit as long as he continued to make small payments, including the growing interest due each month. Unfortunately, the credit card was used for house payments so often that ultimately the unpaid balance reached more than $25,000, with monthly interest payments alone surpassing $500 per month.

Needless to say, the young man finally lost his house and now has to rent from a landlord.

Such a practice should not be permitted for the customer's best interest. With a debt-driven economy such as today's, credit card companies and financial institutions, through advertising, entice some people to go with an economic logic that encourages them to be fiscally irresponsible. With such logic it also becomes easier to be less accountable in other areas of life.

Economic Logic in the Old Testament

In Old Testament times God recognized this tendency to accumulate too much debt. He established unique economic laws that encouraged everyone to be debt free by the end of every sixth year—the beginning of the Sabbatical Year. If that failed, a person could pay off debt by leasing, not selling, his property. The maximum time limit for debt for the entire economy was never to be longer than a forty-nine year period—the beginning of the Jubilee Year— the time when all debt (especially leased land) had to be eliminated. This then would have occurred at least once in every person's working lifetime.

If a farmer got into financial difficulty and he had already indentured himself to work for another person until the end of the next Sabbatical (seven year period), and it was the forty-second year since the last Jubilee (another seven to go until the next), he could "sell" his land to another farmer. The "buyer" in turn could only use the land for the next six years, after which time he would have to return it to its original owner debt free. In reality, value was placed on the use of the land rather than the land itself.

Did the Lord know something that we have overlooked which happens when economic and moral logic separate? A study of the last two centuries reveal that in this country we have had either a deep depression or a severe recession about every fifty years. There was one in 1880, another in 1929, and the last major down turn was in October 1987, when the Dow Jones Industrials lost twenty-three percent of its value in one day. In this last incidence the reckoning was delayed seven years by encouraging debt and easing interest rates. This was done with innovation sometimes. For example, automobile dealers would charge an additional $1000 for a car, then "return it" as if it was a "cash back" to the buyers. This was a neat economic trick to give down-payment-money to those not having it. It kept a depression from coming, but it stimulated a tremendous rise in private debt that still has not abated.

At the time of the writing of this book, a large ad is in the daily newspaper advocating that people "lease" a car rather than buy it. The ad asks, "Why does it make good economic sense to lease a car instead of buying it? Quite simply because it's cheaper." That just is not true! There is a smaller payment each month, but at the end of the lease the buyer owns nothing! He actually has paid out and lost more money than he would have if he had bought it and paid interest each month. He then would have something of value to show for his investment after the payments stop. It is not so with leasing. Leasing instead of buying is not at all "cheaper" but many thousands are doing it. The dealers are pushing it simply because it helps them sell cars to people who are not willing to contract more debt now, but at the expense of having much more later.

A Sinner Disregards His Influence on Others

It is clear that one of Satan's first concerns is to make a sinner give little consideration to what ill effect his actions will have on others, often his own children. He makes him feel he can do whatever he wants without worrying about "influence."

King David apparently believed he could commit his act of adultery without it influencing his children in any way. Yet they copied his sins and may have been encouraged in doing so by their being aware of what he did when they were younger.

First, Amnon took advantage of his half-sister Tamar. Later, Absalom killed Amnon for his crime. David's lack of forgiveness of Absalom seems to have made his son choose to "get even." Absalom nearly succeeded in overthrowing David. Then in time, Adonijah tried to take the throne without David's blessing, which ultimately seems to have brought about his death at the hands of Solomon.

One also wonders what influence David's conduct of having multiple wives had upon Solomon's decision to follow suit and take it to the greatest degree.

King Jehoshaphat, certainly one of the best kings of Judah in the period of the divided monarchy, made that momentous decision to join forces with the evil King Ahab of Israel in the ill-fated battle of Ramoth Gilead. Ahab had been told by the prophet Micaiah that he would die if he fought (1 Kings 22:1-28). Jehoshaphat's son, Jehoram, later married Athaliah, the daughter of the evil Ahab and Jezebel (2 Kings 8:18). That union may have been the way the two kings sealed their treaty, for that was often the custom at the time.

The evil influence of Athaliah on Jehoram led to his causing the death of his six brothers (2 Chronicles 21:4). After Jehoram died, Athaliah, his wife, decided she would take over the throne even though she was not in the Messianic line as a direct descendant of King David. To do so safely, she gave the order that all her grandchildren had to be killed so she could rule uncontested (2 Chronicles 22:10). Jehoram's only son, Ahaziah, was killed while visiting his wounded uncle. It is safe to observe that had it not been for the wise counsel of Jehoiada, the high priest, to save the one-year-old grandson, Joash, from being murdered and hiding him in the temple for six years, the Messianic line of king David would have come to an end.

It is sobering to realize that all this came about as the result of a decision of one of the most godly kings in the entire Old Testament period, Jehoshaphat, to join forces with Ahab at Ramoth Gilead. If only Jehoshaphat had just a glimpse of the effects his decision would have not only on his own family, but on God's ultimate plan for the human race, perhaps biblical history might have taken a different course. He seems rather to have had concern only for himself and with his present situation.

The World's: "I Own" and "I Owe"

Sin causes one to become increasingly self-centered, and less and less others-centered.

I OWN

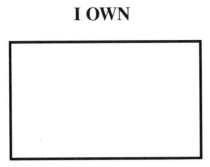

A person can live in one of two worlds: a selfless world or a self-centered world. The latter can best be described as a "Pagan World." It is the world of "I Own." It can be labeled a "square world." It is the world of self-centered fulfillment. Its occupant thinks, "This is my world. I don't owe anyone anything. My own contentment is all-important. I must look out for what I think is best for me."

In life's focus and direction, in outlook and drive, in ends and goals, the person who walks in this world finds *"self"* taking precedence over all else. There is an accompanying disregard for how others will be affected by actions taken. If he steps out of his world, it is only when he assumes he can benefit by it. He wants friends, but friendship is sought only from those who can serve his ultimate purposes, who can make a contribution to *his* life, who can enter his "square."

In time it is but natural for this world to shrink around the person. It ultimately becomes his own prison. Would-be friends soon begin to disappear. They feel used. They recognize that this person's world is a "one way" world, a "give me" world. They come from it feeling drained and are less and less anxious to enter it again. It is not uncommon for the person occupying it to finally say, "Why don't people like me? Why am I so lonely?"

I OWE

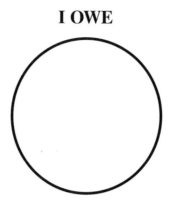

The other world in which one can operate is the "Christian World." It is the world of "I Owe." It is a selfless world. It is a world where people find contentment and fulfillment meeting others' needs in self-sacrificing service. One who walks in it says, "I find greatest fulfillment in helping those who need help. I must look out for what is best for others." He willingly gets out of his circle, not to bring others in, but to take a piece of himself and give it to benefit others.

It is only natural for the world of this person to grow. When he reaches out of his circle, it is to offer a piece of himself and invest it in others. His world expands, enlarges, and he never wants for friendship. He is well liked. His friendship is sought by all and he finds happiness.

The Apostle Paul gives clarity to the need for operating out of the "I Owe" world in his admonition to the Philippians (2:3). "Let nothing be done through selfishness or empty conceit, but with humility of mind let each of you regard one another as more important than himself."

Sin Destroys One's Self-image

It is ironic that a sinner begins his sinful activity with the thought that he is competent enough to make his own decisions. Yet sin eats at the very thing on which all proper decisions rest—self-confidence.

Eve thought she knew easily what was in her best interest. At the moment of her sin, she believed she could rely more on her own judgment with respect to what was best for her than on God's direction.

God had wanted Eve's experience with evil to be entirely academic. She was to learn about the evil effects of sin by being told what it would do, rather than actually doing it herself. When she sinned, she knew sin experientially, something from which God had sought to protect her.

Eve must have said to herself, like all sinners after doing their sinful acts, "Why did I do that? I knew better!" And down went self-respect!

The end result is that the sinner always thinks less of himself than he did before the sin was committed. And the lower one drops in his own estimation, the more normal it seems to sin, and the greater loss of self-respect. Sinful acts seem to multiply in direct relationship to the loss of self worth.

The sinner's self worth continues to drop until no sin seems beneath him.

God Wants Us to Be Maximally Happy

When we are in a hurry to go somewhere, stop signs and red lights, curbs and corners, no passing lanes, and speed limits are hindrances in one sense. We could arrive faster without them. Or could we? They do help us get to our intended destination safely. They keep us from being in an accident, causing injury either to ourselves or to others. These "limitations" (laws) then are in reality our friends. We need them.

The thesis of this book has been quite simply that God gave the Ten Commandments to keep us from injuring ourselves, and sometimes others, not only spiritually but physically, emotionally, and psychologically. He wanted us to have a well-rounded wholeness, a maximum happiness in the future, and not do anything in word or deed that would jeopardize or restrict the fullest expression of our personal fulfillment in life, now or in the future.

There follows a chart that specifies each of the Ten Commandments. Column two gives the purpose of the commandment, the part of life God wanted to preserve for us, followed by column three which briefly sets out the consequences that automatically follow the violation of that commandment.

GOD'S DESIRE FOR OUR MAXIMUM HAPPINESS

God wants to protect our personality, to preserve and ensure happiness. Anything that aims at destroying the sacred quality and well-rounded wholesomeness of life is a capital offense against God, mainly because it hurts us in the long run.

"For I know the plans I have for you, says the LORD. They are plans for good and not for evil, to give you a future and a hope" (Jeremiah 29:11).

COMMANDMENTS STATED	PURPOSE FOR THE COMMANDMENTS	HOW WE HURT OURSELVES BY BREAKING THEM
1. NO OTHER GODS	To maintain wholeness and preserve indentity; internal worship	The unity of life is fractured and the personality is "split;" hypocrisy develops
2. NO IMAGES	To sustain a right relationship with God and preserve external worship	A proper relationship with God is damaged; self becomes a god because it now "creates" gods
3. NO NAME IN VAIN	To avoid self-worship and hold to a proper respect for God	People try to manipulate God; His name becomes a cheap expression; God loses His importance in life
4. SABBATH REMEMBRANCE	To promote worship; make living "holy;" foster genuine friendship	Life becomes secular, loses its meaning; values are confused; respect is seriously eroded
5. HONOR PARENTS	To foster love; reinforce respect for authority	Love decreases; contentment diminishes; abuses increase
6. NO MURDER	To preserve the sanctity of human life	Respect for life lessens; people become "things;" children grow up to become poor parents
7. NO IMMORALITY	To ensure the family unit is kept on the proper moral and spiritual level	The sanctity and unity of the family is weakened and soon destroyed; youth choose the wrong mate; divorce happens; child abuse increases
8. NO STEALING	To protect private property; encourage creativity; develop friendships	Initiative, creativity, and thrift are damaged; property is valued over people
9. NO LYING	To advance credibility, reliability, dependability	Creditability is lost; suspicion grows; trustworthiness suffers
10. NO COVETING	To maintain quality relationships; encourage generosity; discourage selfishness	Relationships are destroyed; attitudes sour; self-centeredness increases; personality is damaged; money becomes a god; one is encouraged to steal

General Observations

Some general observations about the Commandments are in order here to better understand their study.

A. First, these "Ten Words" are found two places in the Old Testament: Exodus 20:1-17 and Deuteronomy 5:1-22. Moses was given the law, the *Torah*, on Mount Sinai and that *Torah* is summed up in the Ten Commandments. These laws were so fundamental to the well-being generally, and over all, that they are given twice for added emphasis.

B. Notice also the statement in Exodus 20:1: "All these words" is deliberately connected to the phrase "And God spoke." The whole stress is that these commandments are words of revelation coming directly from God. The first emphasis is on the *source* from which the words come, the second emphasis is on the *reason* these words are given, and the third emphasis is on *content* (Exodus 20:2-17).

C. Since God is not a God of speculation, He does not express himself in philosophical terms. These ten guidelines are God's will expressed in terms of moral imperatives. The LORD is a God of history, "I . . . brought you out of Egypt" (Exodus 20:2). In verses 3-11, He shows He is also the God of daily life.

D. There seems to be no special reason for the Lord using the number ten. The Hebrews, like most peoples, counted from base ten probably because of ten fingers. The institution of the tithe (Genesis 28:22) shows how this basis of ten could take on a religious meaning. Twelve might have been the more obvious number, since that number is used so often (12 tribes, 12 spies, 12 administrative districts, 12 disciples). It is ironic that the originators of mathematics, the Sumerians, actually had a mathematical system based on the number six.

E. The word "Commandment" does not appear in connection with these laws in the text. They are called "Words." This should help to remove from our minds the harshness often connected with the idea of something that has to be done. This is not to say that a Christian is one so free that he is not required to follow these "Words." Indeed, God did not give them as "Ten Suggestions" which we could take or leave. They are rather the "correct responses" that God's people have.

God intended that these ten guides for attitudes and actions should be basic to those who follow Him. But in the true sense, they are not a list of items that have to be *obeyed* if one is to be considered a follower of God.

Rather, these are the things that followers of God *do*. To put it another way, these are not the rules by which one is permitted to enter the house. They are rather what the people do who are already *in* the house.

It is theoretically possible that one could be abiding by all ten "Words" or statements and still not be a Christian, for doing them simply does not make one "saved." That takes repentance on our part and forgiveness on God's part. However, with our sinful hearts, it is not practically possible to obey these "laws." But they do indeed make one aware of how helpless he is in his own power to keep the standard God has set for him. It takes nothing short of a complete change of heart.

Many, if not most people, abide by today's laws for fear of the punishment that would result if the laws were broken and they got caught. It is the fear of the consequences of law that keeps them law abiding. But what would happen if the consquences or fear was removed?

Imagine for a moment what would happen if the federal legislature enacted a law that after midnight January 1, there would be no more laws passed. All laws on the books would no longer be enforced. Police and sheriff's departments would be closed and no further arrests would be made for any infraction. What do you suppose would happen one minute after the stroke of midnight on that date? All chaos would break loose in society for everyone, except those who have the law *written on their hearts*. Their moral conduct would not vary at all. They would still observe the Ten Commandments because the diamond stylus of grace has penetrated their rock hard hearts, and now they are able to control their actions from within.

It is theoretically possible for a law to be passed that would make a person quit drinking, but there is no law possible that can prevent one from being the kind of person who needs a law to make him quit drinking. One can be prevented from stealing by a law enacted, but there is no law that can be passed that can keep one from being the kind of person that needs a law to keep from stealing.

If a society is to be orderly, it is important that the people do not steal from each other, lie to one another, or commit murder. But it is far more important that the people of that society have a central belief system that gives them the conviction that stealing, lying, and murder are wrong, always wrong, even when they are assured no punishment from society would come to them if they did it.

For people to know what is right is fundamental and critical to an orderly society, but for those people to have the power and courage to do what is right is far more important and far more essential.

This is why grace is far more fundamental than law can ever be. The law can simply tell the sinner how he should act, but without grace he simply lacks the power to make it happen.

The laws did not come down from a big-robed judge, sitting in his lofty chair, with a furrowed forehead, frowning fiercely, gavel in his hand, ready to thunder forth his requirements. They were rather given by God in a most loving spirit, knowing exactly what it would take for men and women to come to Him. These laws best reflect God's own nature and His character. Since His will is for us to be like Him, these ten ingredients are a part of the mix that can make us to be like Him as far as it is humanly possible.

F. It is observed that only the fourth and fifth commandments are stated in a positive form; the other eight are all stated negatively. God could have cast them all in a positive form, but one negative command can take the place of numerous positive commands. In addition, a negative command can be given in fewer words that will more succinctly meet the evil human heart head on.

However, even though stated in a positive way, every moral act required has another negative side which demands that something must not be done. God is not pleased at all with one who simply avoids doing a "do-not-do" thing. One could comply with that requirement by doing nothing at all. It is not inactivity that God wants. It is rather right and moral actions He desires. When God forbids any evil action, it is done with the idea in mind that the opposite good action will take its place.

G. We notice that God's requirements reach deeper than the surface of our actions. He touches the attitudes, the enticements, the pressures, the incentives, and all else that lead to a thing forbidden. In short God is not satisfied until the heart is not only softened by grace, but has also been made pure by the touch of His Spirit. Then the heart is no longer rebelling at doing the right thing.

Areas Covered

Let us now give attention to the areas of life that God wanted to be covered with the Ten Commandments. The following chart indicates that the first three commandments are given to establish right relationship with God. The fourth commandment is to assure a proper regard for work, while the last five are directed to society in general. A right relationship with God makes it much easier to have right relationships with society in general.

CHART ONE

RIGHT RELATIONS WITH GOD	RIGHT RELATIONS WITH WORK	RIGHT RELATIONS WITH SOCIETY
1. NO OTHER GODS	4. REMEMBER THE SABBATH	5. HONOR PARENTS
2. NO IMAGES		6. NO MURDER
3. NO NAME IN VAIN		7. NO IMMORALITY
		8. NO STEALING
		9. NO LYING
		10. NO COVETING

There is yet another way of dividing the commandments. Notice in chart two that both commandments four and five have been placed in the column of right relationship to God. Jesus made clear the importance of family relationships by referring to himself as God's Son, and to God as "Our Father."

CHART TWO

RESPONSIBILITY TO GOD	RESPONSIBILITY TO OTHER PEOPLE
1. NO OTHER GODS	6. NO MURDER
2. NO IMAGES (IDOLS)	7. NO IMMORALITY
3. NO NAME IN VAIN	8. NO STEALING
4. REMEMBER SABBATH	9. NO LYING
5. HONOR PARENTS	10. NO COVETING

"Love the LORD your God
with all your heart
and with all your soul
and with all your mind"
(Matthew 22:37).

"Love your neighbor
as yourself."
(Matthew 22:39).

At the bottom of chart two are found the words spoken by Jesus to the Pharisee who was "an expert in the law" and who asked Jesus which was "the greatest commandment in the Law?" (Matthew 22:34-40). Notice that the first half of the statement summarizes the first five commandments (or four as some would divide them). The last half summarizes the remainder. It is clear to see that in regard to the moral law we have been studying, Jesus did not come to destroy it but to fulfill it.